Praise for

Learning for Careers:
The Pathways to Prosperity Network

"Hoffman and Schwartz's *Leading for Careers* is a must-read for legislators, business partners, and K–12 and higher education leaders who care about preparing young people for careers. The authors provide a thorough and thoughtful summary of how states are taking on the challenge of ensuring more students are career-ready—not just college-ready—and specifically prepared for high-growth and high-demand jobs. Their summary of the impact of the Pathways to Prosperity Network across multiple states, including Tennessee, is inspiring. Kudos to both authors for their leadership in changing the conversation as well as the landscape on the ground in our states."

> **— Candice McQueen, commissioner, Tennessee**
> **Department of Education**

"With a trenchant foreword by Tony Carnevale, this experience-packed, on-point book will sharpen our oft fumbling effort to make real the 'career' part of 'college- and career-ready' and furnish many more young Americans with a rigorous, respectable, and lucrative alternative to the 'four-year degree for all' goal that has ill-served too many kids and misled too many education reformers."

> **— Chester E. Finn, Jr., distinguished senior fellow and**
> **president emeritus, Thomas B. Fordham Institute**

"Pathways to Prosperity is giving thousands of Delaware young people the opportunity to learn valuable skills that will serve them well in the workplace. The best part is seeing how engaged these young people are as they think about their future. We love 'P to P' in Delaware!"

> **— Jack Markell, governor of Delaware (2009–2017)**

"*Learning for Careers* is a must-read for educators, employers, and civic leaders who are partnering to prepare young people for twenty-first-century careers. In developing Here to Here, a scaled career pathway initiative for low-income in-school youth in the South Bronx, we have relied on the exceptional work described in this book. It has been essential to Here to Here's success thus far."

> **— Judy and Jamie Dimon, The James and Judith K.**
> **Dimon Foundation**

"Nancy Hoffman and Bob Schwartz's work constitutes the true definition of education reform in our country. They address one of America's fundamental challenges: How do we make public education much more relevant to the needs of the changing modern workforce? Their work is essential reading for everyone interested in how to smartly combine rigorous academics with real-world application."

> — **Darrell Steinberg, mayor of Sacramento, former president of the California State Senate, and author of the California Career Pathways Trust**

"Career and Technical Education (CTE) reforms are extremely demanding. They must create a robust continuum between the worlds of work and education where actors cooperate intensively with each other. This complex endeavor is even more challenging in the United States due to its extremely fragmented state-level education systems. This book is an absolutely inspiring report for all CTE reform leaders in the world."

> — **Ursula Renold, head of research division education systems, Swiss Economic Institute, ETH Zurich**

"The 1990 report of the Commission on the Skills of the American Workforce strongly recommended that the United States greatly raise academic standards for all students and create a world-class work-based vocational education system. Instead, the United States raised standards for some while wrecking the vocational education system for many. This book describes what the country needs to do to get back on track."

> — **Marc Tucker, president, National Center on Education and the Economy**

LEARNING FOR CAREERS

The Pathways to Prosperity Network

NANCY HOFFMAN
ROBERT B. SCHWARTZ

Harvard Education Press
Cambridge, Massachusetts

Copyright © 2017 by the President and Fellows of Harvard College

All rights reserved. No part of this publication may be reproduced or transmitted in any form or by any means, electronic or mechanical, including photocopy, recording, or any information storage and retrieval systems, without permission in writing from the publisher.

Paperback ISBN 978-1-68253-111-2
Library Edition ISBN 978-1-68253-112-9

Library of Congress Cataloging-in-Publication Data
Names: Hoffman, Nancy, author. | Schwartz, Robert B. (Educator), author.
Title: Learning for careers : the Pathways to Prosperity Network /
    Nancy Hoffman, Robert B. Schwartz.
Description: Cambridge, Massachusetts : Harvard Education Press, [2017] |
    Includes bibliographical references and index.
Identifiers: LCCN 2017024147| ISBN 9781682531112 (pbk.) |
    ISBN 9781682531129 (library edition)
Subjects: LCSH: Young adults—Education—United States. | Young
    adults—Employment—United States. | Education—Economic aspects—
    United States. | Vocational education—United States. | School-to-work
    transition—United States. | Wages—Effect of education on—United States.
Classification: LCC HD6270 .H54 2017 | DDC 362/.0425—dc23 LC
    record available at https://lccn.loc.gov/2017024147

Published by Harvard Education Press,
an imprint of the Harvard Education Publishing Group

Harvard Education Press
8 Story Street
Cambridge, MA 02138

Cover Design: Ciano Design
Cover Photo: laflor/E+/Getty Images

The typefaces used in this book are Adobe Garamond Pro for text and
Futura for display.

CONTENTS

FOREWORD

Two powerful economic trends have driven education reform since the seminal publication of *A Nation at Risk* in 1983.

The first trend, widely celebrated by educators, is that, on average, irrespective of field of study, the wage premium for college degrees over high school diplomas has doubled. That trend implies that, on average, more postsecondary education results in higher earnings irrespective of major field of study. This suggests that the proper goal for policy is the oft-repeated "college for all," with the BA as the gold standard for success and the graduate degree as even better.

The second, and more dramatic, trend is most often ignored by education reformers. That trend shows that while the wage premium for the average BA has doubled, at the same time, the variation in earnings by postsecondary field of study, from the lowest to the highest, has more than quadrupled. This demonstrates that the relationship between fields of study and their connection to particular career pathways has increasingly powerful effects on future earnings. Differences in earnings by field of study is also why oftentimes less education is worth more in a high-paid field of study than more education in a low-paid field of study. It is why more than 40 percent of people with BAs make more than people with graduate degrees; 30 percent of AAs result in higher incomes than the average BA; and many certificate holders make more than the average person with an AA or BA. But until the recent past, education reformers continued to embrace "college for all" and largely ignore the importance of field of study or the value of any postsecondary credential other than the four-year degree.

In 2011, however, with the publication from the Harvard Graduate School of Education (HGSE) of *Pathways to Prosperity*, the tide began to turn. Drawing on data from the Center I lead at Georgetown University and other sources, the Pathways authors challenged the premise that the only path to a middle-class income is through a four-year college or university, and provided compelling evidence from other nations that strong vocational education systems could be engines of economic mobility and growth.

In *Learning for Careers* one of the *Pathways* report authors, Bob Schwartz, along with Nancy Hoffman, documents the extraordinary efforts of a growing number of states and regions that have come together under the umbrella of HGSE and Jobs for the Future (JFF) to tackle the challenge of building career pathways systems designed to provide young people with the combination of academic, social, and technical skills, credentials, and work experience needed to launch them into careers in high-growth, high-demand fields like health care and information technology. The Pathways to Prosperity Network, cofounded by Hoffman and Schwartz in 2012, brings together leaders from government, business, K–12 and higher education, and the workforce system at the state and regional levels to build pathways that span grades 9–14 and are aligned with regional labor market needs. In states as diverse in size and demographics as Arizona, California, Delaware, Massachusetts, Tennessee, and Texas, and regions including Central Ohio, the Twin Cities, and New York City, leaders are working across agencies and sectors to create a visible opportunity structure for a broad cross-section of young people whose needs are not well served by an academics-only diet. The book documents the progress some of the leading states and regions in the Pathways Network are making without at all minimizing the technical and political challenges entailed in trying to strike a better balance between the academic and career purposes of education. The Pathways Network is trying to elevate career readiness, not just college readiness, as an important goal for all students. The importance of the Pathways Network—and of this book, which describes what it has accomplished and points to the work ahead—can scarcely be overstated.

We often forget that the clarion call to education reform in 1983 was primarily a response to an economic threat. It announced: "Our nation is at risk. Our once unchallenged preeminence in commerce, industry, science, and technological innovation is being overtaken by competitors throughout the world . . . (W)hat is at risk is the promise first made on this continent . . . that all children . . . can hope to attain . . . gainful employment."

"Gainful employment" is a far cry from "college for all." In part that disconnect has resulted from the fact that for its first twenty years education reform focused on the academic basics in elementary school, far removed from the nexus of the education pipeline and the economy. But as the reform movement moved up the education ladder toward high school, the need to align education reforms with economic ends has become unavoidable.

The 2005 National Education Summit on High School moved beyond the academic basics toward a reassertion of the "gainful employment" standard for reform: "Building and expanding on past successes, the 2005 National Education Summit on High Schools looks toward an even bolder goal: redefining the role of high school in America while better connecting its curriculum to the expectations of colleges and employers. It takes us to the next level in raising standards and achieving accountability. It is no longer enough to ensure that all students are proficient at each grade level. It is time for every student to graduate both proficient and prepared for the real demands of work and postsecondary learning."

But this reassertion of the gainful employment perspective proved to be way too little and way too late. By 2005 vocational education had already been banished from high school curriculums in favor of a one-size-fits-all academic pedagogy and curriculum designed to move everybody from high school to Harvard. Less than 1 percent of high school students were getting any meaningful occupational preparation.

To their credit the K–12 reformers were intent on providing a solid standards-based academic education for all students. But standards-based academic education has become too much of good thing, especially at the high school level. As the vocational pathways in high school shut down, the academic curriculum rapidly became the only pathway to college and middle-class careers. It has become harder and harder to sell the pure academic pathway when no more than a third of the students are able to make the journey from high school to the BA. Academic reform in high school has also foundered on the shoals of abstraction characteristic of the new academic curriculum. Algebra II, for example, has become, for many, an artificial academic barrier to meaningful learning, not to mention high school and postsecondary completion. Nonetheless, the academic gatekeepers have soldiered on and doubled down on the academic high school with commitment to a nationwide "common core" curriculum.

As Hoffman and Schwartz show, academic standards have their place, but the logic of gainful employment and career pathways refuses to go away. They document why and how career pathways have gradually regained traction in secondary and postsecondary education. After banishment from the high school curriculum, vocational education has changed its name and rejoined the polite conversation in the guise of Career and Technical Education (CTE). There is a host of new entrants—including career academies, early college high schools, internships, apprenticeships, and occupational certificates—to the world of career-oriented programming.

The authors explain why and how our ability to move on with progressive education reforms will depend on our success in crossing four of the great divides between education and the workaday world.

First, at the most general level, we need to bridge the divide between academic and applied pedagogies. The current math, science, and humanities curriculums, for example, are organized as discrete hierarchies of increasing complexity and abstraction. Because they are taught abstractly, they don't take advantage of applied pedagogy and are less accessible to students with an applied orientation and learning style. Both academic and applied learning suffer for want of integration.

Second, we need to bridge the divide between high school and college curriculums. The majority of students step off the disciplinary hierarchy in math, the sciences, English, and the humanities after high school in favor of applied major fields of study. The current focus on an academic core curriculum in high school does not provide an obvious transition to the more applied focus of postsecondary majors and fields of study.

Third, we need to do a better job of crossing the divide between general education and particular career pathways in the interest of advancing both

for all Americans. The current academic curriculum does best at producing academic knowledge and abilities—the kinds of knowledge and abilities
measured by tests like the ACT, SAT, and GRE. Academic education does
not do well at producing career competencies, like problem solving and critical thinking, that are best learned and tested in applied contexts. For example, the current high school math curriculum, which emphasizes arithmetic
through Algebra II, does not match up with the math requirements of the
vast majority of college majors or occupations. Even a casual analysis of the
distribution of occupational skills demonstrates that less than 10 percent of
workers use specific academic operations from geometry, algebra, or calculus
on the job.

Fourth, we need to make sure that career pathways programs help to
reduce, not increase, the class and racial divide in education and economic
opportunity. We need to be sure that pathway programs do not reinforce the
class- and race-based tracking deeply embedded in American society and,
which, unfortunately is the default tendency in American education. The
reforms that began in 1983 were intended to eradicate class- and race-based
tracking by eliminating vocational and academic dumping grounds for the
least advantaged students. Instead, by elevating a single academic pathway
from high school to the BA as the highly preferred, most well-traveled but
least often completed pathway to the middle class, standards-based academic
reforms have encouraged striving among disadvantaged students but have
also helped increase race and class inequality. That's why differences in access
to postsecondary degrees with labor market value have accounted for most of
the historical increase in earnings inequality since it began its dramatic spike
in the early eighties. That's also why Hoffman and Schwartz insist that, while
the focus of their Network's efforts is on getting more young people through
to a first postsecondary credential with labor market value, this must be done
in ways that don't foreclose the opportunity to continue on to a four-year
degree, or more, should a young person wish to do so. Indeed, what we see
so often is that once young people gain a sub-baccalaureate education and
the capacity to enter the labor market in a well-paying job, they have the
confidence and resources to go on to the BA, thus reducing the increasing

dualism in our education system that disproportionately reserves the BA for affluent whites and increasingly relegates minorities and lower-income students to sub-baccalaureate job training.

Ultimately, we need to cross the divide between schooling and career pathways because of the inescapable fact that our society is based on work. Those who are not equipped with the knowledge and skills necessary to get—and keep—good jobs are denied full social inclusion and tend to drop out of the mainstream culture, polity, and economy. In the worst cases, they are drawn into alternative cultures, political movements, and economic activities that are a threat to mainstream American life. Hence, if secondary and postsecondary educators cannot fulfill their economic mission to help youth and adults become successful workers, they also will fail in their cultural and political missions to create lifelong learners, good neighbors, and good citizens. The ultimate relevance of education is when it empowers people to do work in the world rather than retreat from it.

Learning for Careers is a signal contribution to this urgent effort to make education fully relevant to the career and life aspirations of all young people. In their vivid account of how Pathways networks—real collaborations between a range of educational institutions with businesses and political organizations—make it possible for young people to prepare for and embark upon successful, lasting careers, Hoffman and Schwartz summarize exceptionally important work and progress of the last decade while pointing to work that has yet to be accomplished. Their book will remain a touchstone for many education and workplace reformers in the years ahead.

Anthony P. Carnevale
Research Professor and Director
The Georgetown University Center on
Education and the Workforce

INTRODUCTION

The American system for preparing young people to lead productive and prosperous lives as adults is clearly badly broken . . . Building a better network of pathways to adulthood for our young is one of the paramount challenges of our time.

With these words, *Pathways to Prosperity: Meeting the Challenge of Preparing Young Americans for the 21st Century*, a 2011 report from the Harvard Graduate School of Education, sounded an alarm about the narrowing life prospects of millions of young Americans. The United States was failing to prepare young adults to succeed in the workplace or, ultimately, to support themselves and their families. The report's writers, who included one of us (Schwartz), did not use phrases like "badly broken" and "paramount challenges" lightly. But amidst growing anxiety about the rising cost of a college education and doubts about the return on those investments (symbolized by all of the unemployed twenty-somethings living in their parents' basements), the report struck a nerve. The interest the report generated surprised even its authors. Its call to action resonated: employers need to engage more actively with educators and create alternatives to the predominant road to the middle class, which for decades had been a four-year college degree. Establishing a broader set of pathways, beginning in high school and ending in a variety of postsecondary credentials with high value in the labor market, is crucial to enable the two-thirds of young adults without a four-year degree to get the skills, knowledge, and work experience they need in order to launch themselves into successful, well-paying careers.

Fortunately, the United States did not need to start from scratch. Surprising as it was to many readers, one of the report's key observations was that other countries were doing much better in preparing youth for the world of work. These countries—northern and central European nations especially—had comprehensive vocational education *systems* that were attractive to a large number and wide range of students. They offered teenagers multiple meaningful job experiences, provided substantial flexibility and choice, and resulted in smooth transitions into the labor market.

That vision provides the frame for the work chronicled in this book—the creation of a national network of states, metropolitan regions, and large cities focused on developing systems of career pathways that span grades 9–14 and equip young people with the foundation required to start careers in such high-growth fields as information technology and health care. We launched the Pathways to Prosperity Network in 2012 as a collaboration between our respective organizations, the Harvard Graduate School of Education (HGSE) and Jobs for the Future (JFF), a Boston-based national nonprofit that builds educational and economic opportunity for underserved populations in the United States. We are now five years into the work, far enough along to be able to celebrate the early successes of some of our Network members. At the same time, we have become even more aware of just how daunting the challenges are in attempting to design and implement career pathways systems that cross two long-standing American divides—the gap between secondary and postsecondary education as well as the gap between what education provides and employers say they need. Today the case for bridging those gaps is, if anything, stronger than it was in 2012.

In the run-up to and the aftermath of the 2016 presidential election, Americans heard endlessly about the people and places the economic recovery left behind. We heard about stagnant wages and disgruntled, disaffected adults who were out of work or underemployed. We heard story after story about regions of the United States with high numbers of non-college-educated workers who were struggling to stay afloat financially. And we heard about manufacturing jobs lost to the global marketplace. But we heard barely a word about education and nothing at all about the condition of young people who were at risk in the uneven economy. Yet youth, too, belong to the dispossessed. The recession had an inordinately heavy impact on our young people, especially young people of color, youth from low-income backgrounds, and youth who either dropped out of high school or graduated but have no postsecondary education plans. The rising number of young people ages sixteen to twenty-four who were out of school and out of work did not attract attention. Nor did the college graduates with four-year degrees who couldn't find decent jobs—an anomaly compared with recoveries in the past.

Although the economic prospects of young Americans were not a significant issue in the 2016 political campaign, their situation has been receiving increasing attention among national organizations concerned about education and workforce development, among state and local leaders, and among a growing group of employers. At a time when education has never been more important to economic success, these stakeholders are struck today by the same three conditions highlighted in the *Pathways* report: falling educational attainment and achievement compared to other nations, a "skills gap" for jobs that pay a middle-class wage, and a dramatic decline in the ability of adolescents and young adults to find work that pays a living wage.

Within the education community, the decades-old "college for all" mantra has been replaced with the goal for all students to leave high school "college and career ready." This shift reflects an acknowledgment that all students could benefit from more exposure to the world of work before they arrive at adulthood, and that college should not be viewed as a destination but rather as a pathway leading to a set of career options. State and local leaders, and governors in particular, are speaking out about the economic importance of better tailoring education to the new high-skill economy. There is a growing realization among employers that in order to meet their talent needs, they will have to engage with the education community in a more serious way. This is especially true for the hard-to-fill middle-skill jobs that employers reference when they complain about the skills gap. This understanding is reflected in the initiatives of the US Chamber of Commerce Foundation focused on helping employers apply the principles of supply-chain management to the recruitment, training, and development of their most important resource, their people. It also can be seen in the corporate philanthropy of major firms—like JPMorgan Chase, IBM, and SAP—that invest in innovative grant programs to help schools and communities do a better job of preparing young people for the new economy.

This book is an early report from the field of an ambitious multistate initiative to change the way young Americans are prepared for careers. The Pathways to Prosperity Network reflects a growing movement in the United States to elevate the status of career preparation in our high schools and colleges, and to challenge the old dichotomy between college and career. In the twentieth century, high schools were organized on the premise that only some students would be going to college while most would be heading directly into the labor market. In the twenty-first century, it is now clear that all young people will need some form of postsecondary education or training if they are going to have a shot at a career that will enable them to support a family. But it is also clear that all young people must leave high school with a much better understanding of the world of work and careers, and a plan for acquiring the skills and credentials to get started on a career. A college degree by itself is no longer a guaranteed ticket to the middle class.

Consequently, while our work is certainly designed to support strengthening and modernizing career and technical education (CTE), it is about more than that. Only about one in five US high school students is a CTE concentrator (meaning the student takes three CTE courses in a single field), but all students need exposure to the world of work.[1] When the authors were growing up, nearly all young people had access to work during their teenage years, in the summers and after school. In the first decade of this century, the proportion of sixteen- and seventeen-year-olds with work experience dropped from just under half to only about one-quarter. But young people from professional families were three times as likely to find work as those from families in poverty. Thus the same young people who might benefit most from a job are the least likely to have one. This tells us that unless high schools take some responsibility for working with employers and community-based organizations to provide internships or other kinds of work experience for the youth who most need it, these young people are likely to join the ranks of the 3 million sixteen- to twenty-four-year-olds who are neither in school nor work and therefore likely to wind up at the back of the hiring queue.[2]

As you will see in the following chapter summaries, we devote much more attention to the role of work in teenagers' lives than is typically the case in books about education. We do this for two reasons. The first is that, in contrast to other organizations focused on one or another form of career education, our goal is not simply to use work and career as an engagement or motivation strategy to get more young people to complete high school, worthy as that is. Our goal is to help young people launch successfully into the labor market with in-demand skills and credentials. This requires seeing them through to a postsecondary certificate or degree. Attaining a first job on a career path that has meaningful advancement potential is the metric that counts most for us, for this is our best hope for breaking the cycle of poverty and economic immobility that has trapped far too many young Americans.

The second reason we focus so much on work is because we believe that work is a critical element in helping young people develop a sense of purpose and a place in the world and the sense of agency to make an impact. Simply put, the Pathways to Prosperity Network is about equipping young people with the skills and experience to make a successful transition not only from school to career, but also from adolescence to young adulthood. Hence, we pay significant attention to youth development as a central element in our work.

At this writing, the Pathways Network includes eight states, Arizona, California, Delaware, Illinois, Indiana, Massachusetts, Tennessee, and Texas; three regions, metropolitan Madison (Wisconsin), central Ohio, and the Twin Cities; and two large cities, New York City and Philadelphia. The number of students participating is ever changing. But thousands of young people are learning and gaining work experience in the Network, ranging from rural youth working in highly mechanized agriculture in California's Central Valley to suburban teens enjoying their school's partnership with high-tech enterprises around Boston to urban youth in Oakland practicing to become EMTs.

In the chapters that follow, we attempt to give a realistic as well as forward-looking portrait of the career pathways movement. In that spirit, we want to be sure to credit the multiple important players in this space. The *Pathways* report profiled several well-established national education organizations with solid track records of providing quality career-related education to high school students—organizations like the National Academy Foundation (now NAF), Project Lead the Way, and the Southern Regional Education Board's High Schools That Work. They continue their important work today, along with several other national education, policy, and business groups that have joined the effort more recently, including the Council of Chief State School Officers, Advance CTE, National Governors Association, and Business Roundtable. While we gratefully acknowledge their contributions and provide some details of their progress, we tell this story with an unabashed focus on the work we know best and from which we've learned the most—the Pathways to Prosperity Network.

Chapter 1 details the evidence that the system we've got for helping young people transition from school into the labor market with relevant skills and credentials in fact remains "badly broken" today. We provide updated data illustrating how the situation harms not only millions of individual young people, with and without high school diplomas, but also employers and the economy as a whole.

Chapter 2 focuses on the origins of the Pathways to Prosperity Network, whose central mission is to help member states and regions design and build career pathways systems. We show what we mean by *career pathways system*—one that enables young people to get started on a career path in a high-growth, high-demand occupational field while still in high school; seamlessly connect to a postsecondary certificate or degree program in that same field; and exit with the skills, credentials, and work experience necessary to launch into the labor market, while leaving open the option to continue their education later if they want to earn a further degree. This chapter outlines the framework, core principles, and evidence base the JFF Pathways team brings to its work with each member, and highlights the three key building blocks that undergird the Network's design.

Chapter 3 illustrates what our work actually looks like on the ground, using vignettes from some of our most developed member states and regions. We provide more detail about how states begin their Pathways work, and how our efforts build upon, but are not limited to, what has traditionally been thought of as vocational education or, more recently, CTE.

Chapter 4 probes more deeply into a core rationale for the Pathways project noted earlier: the importance of introducing work into the lives of young people, particularly for those from low-income families. We look first at the relationship between youth unemployment, economic mobility, and inequality. The chapter then reviews the developmental gains to be had for all young people from activities that take them into the world of work. Apprentice-like experiences help youth gain agency and join multigenerational professional networks. Finally, we make the case that skills and a credential are needed not only for success, but also social capital. Work experiences can help low-income youth develop the networks and connections they need to make good use of their credentials.

Chapter 5 builds on the previous chapter's case for early work experience and describes the Pathways Network's approach to providing early information, awareness, and exposure to the world of work and careers, culminating in an internship or other form of extended work-based learning. Although our main focus in the network is on grades 9–14, in this chapter we argue for beginning at least as early as the middle grades to introduce a systematic, grade-by-grade approach to the world of careers in order to ensure that all students graduate high school "career ready," not just "college ready."

Chapter 6 focuses on two implementation levers that we see as interconnected and mutually reinforcing: the engagement of employers and the development of intermediary organizations. If there is a single factor that most differentiates the international high performers in this field from the United States, it is the role that employers play. In countries like Switzerland, Germany, and Austria, employers are active partners with educators and government officials in shaping the system. Intermediary organizations, sitting between education institutions and employers, make important contributions in mobilizing employer resources to help schools strengthen career preparation.

State policies supporting pathways are also critical to implementation—enabling, yet not ensuring, success. Chapter 7 addresses the evolution of policies that encourage and support the integration and alignment of high school and college learning, as well as work-based learning experiences. While US education leaders long have talked about a seamless K–16 system, the disconnect across high school and college persists, with far too many obstacles in the way of students' smooth transition between the systems.

In chapter 8, the conclusion, we reflect on the state of the growing career pathways movement and ask a fundamental question: Are we and our colleagues building a career pathways *field* as well as a movement? We discuss the common vision movement members hold, but also look ahead to what work we need to do together to build a field with shared identity, shared standards, and deeper grassroots support. Finally, we look ahead at the major challenges facing our Network, and likely other networks as well, in the next five years. We conclude with optimism, but also with the knowledge that this work requires persistence and is not for the faint of heart.

Our work, as you'll see in the chapters ahead, has been significantly influenced by what we have seen and learned in other countries with much better developed systems to help the majority of young people make a successful transition from the world of schooling to the world of work. While being fully mindful of all of the reasons why it is impossible to simply transplant successful education programs from one political and cultural context to another, we remain convinced that there *are* lessons from higher performing vocational systems that can be adapted and applied to the US setting. The Swiss vocational system, in particular, represents for us an "existence proof" that it is possible to design a system that simultaneously meets the developmental needs of young people, provides a wide range of employers with a steady stream of highly skilled young professionals, and enables the nation's economy to remain a world leader.

The fact that the Pathways to Prosperity Network and other national organizations are now paying increased attention to the skills gap is a reflection of growing public concern about whether our education system is designed to meet the needs of a quickly transforming economy. The emerging career pathways movement is a response to that concern, and as such, is attracting support from corporate and philanthropic leaders and from policy makers and elected officials across the political spectrum. In a highly polarized national political environment, a strategy that holds out the promise of being able to better meet the needs of young people and of our rapidly changing economy could become one of the few public policy initiatives with the potential to gain broad bipartisan support.

CHAPTER 1

THEN AND NOW

From *The Forgotten Half* to *Pathways to Prosperity*

What is the purpose of high school? This question, which has been debated for more than a century, lies at the heart of our pathways work. Public high schools emerged in the late 1800s as academic preparation for college, primarily for the elite. High schools first added vocational education and other options for the non-college-bound when enrollment started to soar in the early 1900s. With the decline of manufacturing and expansion of the service sector in the second half of the century, however, college became the preferred route to good jobs that paid a family-supporting wage. By 2008, when Robert Schwartz and two Harvard colleagues began the conversations that led to the publication of *Pathways to Prosperity: Meeting the Challenge of Preparing Young Americans for the 21st Century*, "college for all" was a well-established catchphrase.[1] How did we come to the more recent conclusion that high school should prepare every single student for college *and careers*? The reasons are complicated and reside in recent education reform history. We begin this chapter with a quick look back at the environment in which the *Pathways* report was written and the Pathways to Prosperity Network was born, then bring the story up to date with the work's ongoing relevance today.

Most observers date the start of the current education reform era—arguably the most sustained period of education reform in the nation's history—as 1983, the year in which *A Nation at Risk* was released. The product of a national commission appointed by then–US Education Commissioner T. H. Bell, the report warned in highly dramatic language that the declining performance of our schools threatened America's ability to compete in an increasingly global economy. To quote one of its most famous sentences: "If an unfriendly foreign power had attempted to impose on America the mediocre educational performance that exists today, we might well have viewed it as an act of war."[2] Although the primary evidence cited to support the Commission's claims later came under attack, its recommendations to raise academic standards, strengthen the core curriculum in high schools, and impose more standardized testing were widely embraced. Over the next couple of years, the overwhelming majority of states passed laws aimed at implementing the recommended changes.

A wave of policy reports followed from other national commissions and organizations, including the Carnegie Forum's *A Nation Prepared*, which focused on strengthening the teaching profession, and *Time for Results*, a call from the nation's governors for more accountability from the education community in return for regulatory relief.[3] Only one challenged the unstated premise of the Commission's work: namely, that the principal job of American high schools is to prepare young people for college. It was called *The Forgotten Half: Non-College Youth in America*.[4]

The Forgotten Half, the product of a W. T. Grant Foundation Commission chaired by another former US Education Commissioner, Harold Howe, focused on eighteen- to twenty-four-year-olds who were not headed to college. The report urged policy makers to provide a much stronger set of education and training programs to enable these young adults to make a successful transition from high school into the world of work. By most social and economic indicators, the young people not in college were at a significant disadvantage compared to those enrolled in postsecondary education. As a country, we were spending only one public dollar on non-college-bound youth for every ten dollars spent on those in college. We needed a serious strategy to help these adolescents become self-sufficient adults. Unfortunately, it wasn't until 1994 that Congress enacted the first major legislation focused explicitly on this challenge—the School-to-Work Opportunities Act. It came with a modest appropriation ($287 million) and a provision to sunset after five years.

THE STANDARDS MOVEMENT OVERSHADOWS
THE SCHOOL-TO-WORK MOVEMENT

The big story of education reform in the 1990s was the rise of the academic standards movement, touched off by the adoption of a first-ever set of National Education Goals by the nation's governors in 1990 and accelerated by the work of an organization established in 1996 by a coalition of corporate leaders and governors, Achieve, Inc. As it happens, one of us (Schwartz) became the first president of Achieve and had a close-up view of the rapid spread of the standards movement and its overshadowing of the school-to-work movement, which was just beginning to take hold.

Simply put, as virtually all states put in place new academic standards in the core academic subjects, assessments at key grade levels to measure annual progress against those standards, and accountability systems designed to enable state intervention in persistently failing schools, rising accountability pressures in many high schools crowded out space for career-focused electives, internships, and other forms of work-based learning. High-stakes testing in reading and math led many urban high schools to double the amount of time devoted to these subjects for struggling students, reducing the opportunity for these students to experience the very kinds of field-based learning activities that might have motivated them to see the relevance of learning the core academic subjects. One measure of the decline in career-related course taking is that between 1982 and 1998 the percentage of high school students taking three or more courses in a single vocational area—the definition of a CTE concentrator—declined from 34 percent to 19 percent.[5]

The bottom line was that by the twentieth anniversary of *The Forgotten Half*, the narrowly academic purposes of high schools had so swamped the career preparation purposes that the new mantra had become "college for all." Despite growing rhetoric that all students were to leave high school "college and career ready," the reference to careers was understood by most to be a throwaway, a bow in the direction of the CTE community. Virtually all of the policy attention was on "college ready." This was the political context in

2008 when Schwartz and two colleagues came together to discuss the possibility of collaborating on a project to address the need for renewed attention to the career purposes of education.

PATHWAYS TO PROSPERITY FOR THE FORGOTTEN HALF

Was there still a "forgotten half" in 2008? That was one big question on the table for the Harvard trio—Kennedy School economist Ronald Ferguson, best known for his work on the racial achievement gap; William Symonds, a journalist who covered education for *Business Week* and was in residence at the Kennedy School; and Schwartz, who was at the time academic dean at the Graduate School of Education. On the face of it, this seemed unlikely, for high schools no longer divided their students into two separate groups, the college bound and the work bound. But the numbers told a different story.

In surveys of high school seniors on their post-graduation plans, over 90 percent said they were going on to some form of postsecondary education. When those same high school graduates were surveyed the following October, roughly two-thirds were in fact enrolled in a postsecondary institution. But when we looked at the proportion of young Americans who had attained a college degree by their mid-twenties, we found a more sobering answer. Only 28 percent had earned a four-year degree or better. Adding on the 10 percent of college graduates with a two-year degree and another 10 percent with a one-year postsecondary occupational certificate with value in the labor market, the total percentage of young people with a meaningful postsecondary credential was just under 50 percent.[6]

This finding raised a crucial question: What is our national strategy to help this other half of young Americans who have no postsecondary credentials at a time when the value of such credentials certifying in-demand skills is rising inexorably? While these young people may not exactly have been "forgotten," it seemed clear to the report's authors that their plight was not getting anywhere near the public policy attention it deserved.

SEEKING SKILLS, SEEKING JOBS: EMPLOYERS, YOUNG WORKERS, AND THE FUTURE OF MIDDLE-SKILL JOBS

One reason schools had become so focused on four-year colleges and universities as the preferred destination for all students is that, for the previous twenty years, economists had been warning that the middle of our economy was "hollowing out." Predictions warned that middle-skill jobs were disappearing. We were headed for a world in which there would be only two kinds of work: high-skill, high-wage jobs requiring at least a four-year degree, and low-skill, low-wage jobs requiring only a high school diploma. With the well-documented decline of the manufacturing sector and the rise of a knowledge-based economy, parents understandably did not want their children to be left behind. When our generation was growing up, only one job in three required anything beyond a high school diploma. In the economy for which our children are being prepared, two jobs in three require postsecondary education.[7]

However, in 2010, as the *Pathways* report team looked more closely at the data, we became increasingly convinced that predictions of the disappearance of middle-skill jobs were premature. We were particularly struck by the work of economist Anthony Carnevale and his colleagues at the Georgetown Center on Education and the Workforce (CEW). The Georgetown CEW estimated that roughly 30 percent of the jobs in 2020 would be in the middle-skill category, certainly requiring education and credentials beyond high school, but not necessarily a four-year degree. The best of these jobs— technicians in fields like information technology (IT), engineering, and health care—had median annual wages of over $50,000 and opportunities for career advancement.[8]

Juxtaposing the degree attainment data of twenty-somethings with the projected educational requirements for middle-skill jobs in the year 2020 enabled us to explain to readers of our *Pathways* report the growing concern among employers about the significance of the skills gap they saw. If two-thirds of the projected jobs available will require some form of postsecondary education or training, but only half of young Americans have such credentials, that would seem to be a big problem. But here again, the economics community was divided. Many economists dismissed the claims of employers, affirmed in survey after survey, that they simply are unable to find qualified workers to fill vacant positions, especially in advanced manufacturing and other sectors with substantial numbers of technician-level, middle-skill jobs. The response of skeptics was that if there were in fact a skills gap, employers would address the problem either by raising wages or investing in training, neither of which they seem willing to do. The fact that employers prefer to hire temps or contract workers or even leave vacancies unfilled rather than paying more or investing in training suggests to the skeptics that employers are crying wolf.

Our understanding of the middle-skill labor market has subsequently been enriched by a 2014 report by Joseph Fuller of Harvard Business School and colleagues from Accenture and Burning Glass, entitled *Bridge the Gap: Rebuilding America's Middle Skills*. Fuller and his colleagues provide a useful working definition of the middle-skill jobs we should focus on from within the larger universe of jobs requiring some education beyond high school but not necessarily a four-year degree. They propose three criteria: jobs that add high value for US businesses, jobs that can lead to upward career mobility, and jobs that are persistently hard to fill. Using real-time labor market data, they differentiate between occupations like technical sales or sales management—where jobs are plentiful, pay well, and meet their three criteria, but for which there are few community college or other training programs—versus occupations that receive substantial attention from policy makers and education and training providers but fail to meet one or more of their criteria. They argue, for example, that a pharmacy technician might seem like an attractive middle-skill job, but it offers little long-term opportunity because, unfortunately, it has no career ladder associated with it. Fuller and colleagues make a powerful case for employers to become more proactive in addressing their middle-skill needs, arguing that they need to bring the same logic and discipline to addressing their talent supply needs as they do to the development of materials supply chains.[9]

While some economists still debate whether there is in fact a skills gap in the United States, the fact that employers keep telling us they can't find job candidates with the skills they need while millions of young people are looking for work argues for a better way of matching supply and demand. Fortunately, there are lessons to be learned from countries all over central and northern Europe that have figured out how to do this and, as a consequence, have robust economies, highly skilled workforces, and vanishingly low rates of youth unemployment. The *Pathways* report drew heavily on two 2010 international reports from the Organization for Economic Cooperation and Development, *Learning for Jobs* and *Jobs for Youth*, to make a case for vocational programs that combine work and learning, and more generally for the power of work-based learning.[10] The challenge raised by the *Pathways* report is this: Can we in the United States realign our education system to better prepare more young people to take advantage of the career opportunities presented by the continuing availability of good middle-skill jobs in high-growth, high-demand fields like those mentioned here—jobs that can put people on a path to economic self-sufficiency?

THE RESPONSE TO THE REPORT: A CALL FOR PATHWAYS

The three authors released the *Pathways* report in February 2011 at an event hosted by the American Youth Policy Forum (AYPF) in Washington, DC. As its title suggests, AYPF is the national organization most focused on trying to keep youth policy issues on the national government's agenda. Its founder, Samuel Halperin, was the executive director and lead author of *The Forgotten Half* two decades earlier, and his presence at the event provided a powerful link between the two reports. US Education Secretary Arne Duncan, a strong advocate for the reform and modernization of CTE from his days as CEO of the Chicago Public Schools, spoke at the event, which helped ensure media attention. He was followed by a lively panel discussion among an urban school superintendent (Andres Alonso from Baltimore), a community college president (Robert Templin from Northern Virginia Community

College), and a leading employer (Stanley Litow from IBM). The panel was designed to illustrate the kind of collaboration required to act on the report's recommendations.

Hardly a week goes by without the release of a new national education-related report, so it is always difficult to predict which reports will get picked up by the press and which ones will languish unattended. For reasons that are still not fully clear to the authors, the *Pathways* report received more attention than most. It generated some controversy within the Washington Beltway, especially from people who feared that it might inadvertently provide encouragement to those who want to back away from common high academic standards for all, or who want to return to an era when vocational students were kept in separate tracks. Outside of Washington, DC, however, the report generated so many speaking requests that the project's one staff member and lead author, William Symonds, was on the road virtually full time for the next year, speaking to governmental, business, and education organizations in over thirty states. The publicity also generated speaking requests from governmental organizations in Australia, Canada, England, New Zealand, and Switzerland.

Our best guess is that there were at least three reasons why the report generated so much interest. First, it was highly readable for a broad audience, having been written primarily by a journalist and thus not in academic jargon. The authors managed to find a language to communicate what a lot of people had been thinking: namely, that the "college for all" mantra, however laudable an aspiration, was allowing policy makers and the public to avert their eyes from the fact that fewer than one young person in three was actually attaining a four-year degree. If our colleges and universities were effectively serving less than a third of our young people, why, we asked, should they be dictating the high school program of study that *all* students should be expected to follow?

A second reason the report resonated is that it came from a "brand" institution: the Harvard Graduate School of Education. While the authors might like to think that the analysis and ideas embedded in the report were sufficiently powerful to carry the day on their own, the fact that the report came from a prestigious institution outside the CTE community provided much of its currency. Given the stigma still associated with anything vocational among elites in this country—best exemplified by the oft-heard remark, "Vocational education is a wonderful thing . . . for other people's children"— having an elite, highly selective higher education institution provide external validation of the work that vocational educators do every day generated an enormous sense of pride and gratitude within that community.

Finally, and perhaps most important, the report played into the growing anxiety among parents and policy makers about the rising costs of four-year colleges and universities, and the no-longer-guaranteed financial return on that investment. In 2011, there was substantial media attention paid to the plight of young college graduates working as servers in restaurants and returning home to live with their families, but little hard data to indicate how widespread this phenomenon was. In 2014, however, the Federal Reserve Bank of New York released a report confirming the basis for such parental anxiety about the return on investment to a four-year degree. That report indicated that 44 percent of young four-year degree holders were underemployed, working involuntarily in part-time jobs or in full-time jobs that traditionally did not require so much education. An additional 9 percent were unemployed.[11]

Meanwhile, Carnevale and his colleagues at the Georgetown CEW were reporting surprising evidence of the returns to different types of postsecondary credentials. While it remains generally true that the more education you have, the higher your lifetime earnings, nearly one-third of those with two-year degrees were earning more than the average four-year-degree holder.[12] The key was the program of study and how well the skills learned align with labor market demands—not the amount of time spent in college. For example, the Georgetown CEW reported that 43 percent of young workers with occupational licenses were outearning the average associate's degree recipient, and 27 percent with licenses were outearning the average bachelor's degree holder.[13] A striking example came from Florida, where two-year technical degree graduates outearned the average bachelor's degree recipient by about $11,000 in the years 2007–2011.[14] It is important to acknowledge international evidence that, whatever the initial advantage that those with vocational credentials might have over university graduates, over time that advantage disappears. However, a recent look in Colorado at returns to different majors and degrees ten years after graduation suggests that, in some technical fields at least, the relative advantage of two-year degrees holds up over time.[15]

In order to convince parents and the public that college continues to be a good investment, economists are especially fond of data comparing the earnings of those with only a high school diploma to those with a four-year degree. As figure 1.1 shows, the gap has been steadily widening for decades and now is approaching twice what it was in 1979.

The big story in these data, however, is not the growth in earnings of college graduates, which was quite modest for a thirty-three-year period. The more important point is the decline (of nearly $4,300) in the real earnings of those with only a high school diploma.

This suggests that for the purpose of evaluating return on educational investment, the most relevant comparison may not be between four-year-degree holders and high school graduates, but rather between those with a four-year degree and those with other, less expensive and time-consuming forms of postsecondary education. For example, the Federal Reserve Bank of New York argues that the return on investment to two- and four-year degrees is about the same—15 percent—and has been so for decades.[16] Given an average student loan debt burden of about $27,000, the no-longer-certain economic returns to a four-year degree, and emerging evidence that those with "some college" (i.e., college dropouts) fare no better in the labor market than those with only a high school diploma, it shouldn't surprise us that parents are increasingly asking whether pursuing a four-year degree is necessarily the best option for their own child. Consequently, policy makers have become increasingly open to the need to build alternative pathways to postsecondary education and training alongside the dominant four-year college pathway. The Pathways to Prosperity Network is one strong manifestation of this growing interest among state and local policy makers.[17]

FIGURE 1.1   Rising earnings disparity between young adults with four-year college degrees and with high school diplomas. Median annual earnings, full-time workers aged 25–32 in 2012 dollars

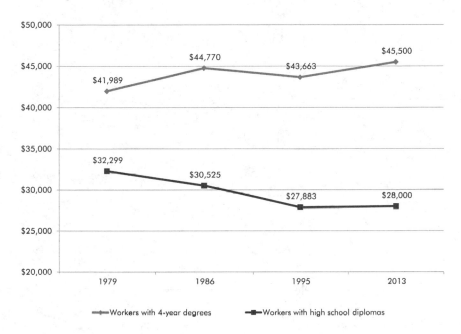

Workers with 4-year degrees   Workers with high school diplomas

Source: Adapted from Pew Research Center, *The Rising Cost of Not Going to College* (Washington, DC: Pew Research Center, 2014).

CHAPTER 2

THE PATHWAYS TO PROSPERITY NETWORK

Origins, Building Blocks, and Framework

Within a few weeks of the release of the *Pathways* report, it became evident that policy makers wanted to take action to address the challenges the report highlighted—if only they knew how. A common refrain Schwartz heard from state education leaders went something like this, "Okay, you've convinced us there is a serious problem in our having been so focused on four-year college as the only acceptable destination after high school, but your report is very light on recommendations. Can you help us figure out what to do?"

This chapter explains the road that led to the Pathways to Prosperity Network of today, with grade 9–14 pathways under development in multiple regions in fourteen states. We describe the origin story of the Network stemming from the *Pathways* report, the lessons learned from the international systems we've seen in action, the education designs in the United States we used as building blocks, and, finally, the framework we created to guide our work.

THE ORIGIN OF THE PATHWAYS NETWORK

Months before the report's release in 2011 Schwartz approached Marlene Seltzer, then president and CEO of Jobs for the Future (JFF), to ask whether the organization would be interested in collaborating with him and his Harvard colleagues if the report generated sufficient interest in the field to warrant follow-up activity. For Schwartz, Boston-based JFF was the obvious organization to reach out to. The thirty-four-year-old nonprofit, which focuses on building educational and economic opportunity for low-income youth and adults, had substantial experience in leading multistate education initiatives for major national funders. Most relevant, JFF was national lead for the Bill & Melinda Gates Foundation's Early College High School Initiative, an innovative model integrating secondary and postsecondary education that was to be a crucial building block for the pathways work ahead. Although Schwartz's connection to JFF goes back almost to its founding, it was only strengthened in 2001 when his wife, Nancy Hoffman, joined the organization and soon thereafter became the vice president responsible for leading the Early College High School Initiative.

In early 2012, Schwartz and Hoffman invited leaders in six interested states to apply to form a network focused on building out statewide systems of career pathways. These systems would integrate high school, community college, and work-based learning with the goal of propelling students to earn not only diplomas, but also career-focused postsecondary credentials of high value to regional employers in such high-growth, high-demand fields as IT, health care, and advanced manufacturing. The pathways would combine rigorous academics (including STEM subjects—science, technology, engineering, and math), technical skills, workplace knowledge, work experience, and the personal and social behaviors that enable a young person to find employment in a first career. Students would have the opportunity to begin taking college-level courses during high school, an accelerated schedule that could help them complete the equivalent of up to two years of college in far less time.

One of the invited states, Illinois, had announced its own pathways initiative even before the invitation was sent, and so was well primed to join. Four other states—Massachusetts, Missouri, North Carolina, and Tennessee— invited Schwartz and/or Hoffman to present to a key group of state leaders from government, K–12 and higher education, business, and the nonprofit and philanthropic sectors prior to deciding whether to apply. In order to ensure that states were genuinely committed to addressing the problems laid out in the *Pathways* report, the newly minted Pathways to Prosperity

Network was designed to be mostly self-financing, with each member state asked to contribute $100,000 per year for three years. In return, the Pathways team, staffed by JFF and HGSE, would provide each state with a set of customized technical assistance and advisory services. The team also would bring leadership teams from each state together in semi-annual institutes focused on addressing core implementation issues and promoting cross-state learning. Finally, the Pathways team committed to raising national funds to support initiatives to benefit all Network members.

The formal launch of the Pathways to Prosperity Network was in October 2012 at the first Pathways Institute at Harvard. The five aforementioned states were each represented by cross-agency, cross-sector teams, as was Long Beach, California, a community so enamored of the career pathways model that it paid its own way to participate even though its state had not yet joined the Network. At the Institute participants were introduced to the Pathways framework and to the broad goals of the Network as well as to the international evidence cited in the *Pathways* report. A highlight of the Institute was the participation of two key leaders from Switzerland—Ursula Renold, who for many years led the federal office overseeing the Vocational Education and Training (VET) system, and Stefan Wolter, an economist whose research on the costs and benefits to employers of providing apprenticeships to young people is widely cited in the field.

EUROPEAN VOCATIONAL EDUCATION MODELS[1]

In Austria, Finland, Germany, the Netherlands, the Nordic countries, and Switzerland, one can see coherent vocational systems designed to help large cohorts of young people make a successful transition from upper secondary school to work. Although the design of these systems differs from country to country, there are some common elements. These systems all serve a broad range of students, between 30 and 70 percent of the age cohort. They all offer pathways leading to credentials in a broad range of occupations, not just the typical blue-collar trades that we in the United States associate with apprenticeships. They all combine learning at the workplace with aligned academic coursework in a classroom setting. They all have substantial employer involvement in curriculum design in order to ensure that the credentials graduates earn will have currency in the labor market. And all of these systems provide some options for graduates to continue on to further education if they choose.

It is easy for American policy makers to tick off the reasons why such systems can't (or shouldn't) be built in the United States. These systems depend on early tracking. They expect students to make binding career choices at too early an age. They require a degree of centralized planning that the United States would never tolerate. They are built on trade and craft traditions that we don't share. Their employers have strong incentives to participate, in part because their labor markets are more regulated than ours. Our unions would never agree to youth sub-minimum wages. The list goes on.

While most of these concerns have some basis in reality in one or more of these systems, they do not characterize the best European systems today. For example, Finland and Denmark demonstrate that one can have a high-quality upper-secondary vocational system without early tracking. Denmark asks students to choose initially from twelve occupational clusters, and only later do students zero in on a more specific occupation. And while Germany struggles to help immigrants succeed, young people born outside of Switzerland do well in that country's vocational system. While it is true that the German labor market is highly regulated, the Swiss labor market operates much like ours, and Switzerland's apprenticeship system is if anything even more impressive than Germany's. Switzerland also has the lowest youth unemployment in Europe. And none of these systems treat the apprenticeship contract as irrevocable; in fact, about 20 percent of German apprentices switch occupations after the first year.

We got to know European vocational education well through our work on various projects for the international Organization for Economic Cooperation and Development (OECD), especially as participants in a sixteen-country study beginning in 2007 called *Learning for Jobs*. European vocational education provided a vision for us of what career-focused education can look like when it is intended to launch most young people into a first career.

In our OECD visits in the Nordic countries as well as the Netherlands, Germany, and most notably Switzerland, we had seen that large numbers of young people chose vocational upper-secondary school as an alternative to the purely academic track leading to university. Vocational upper-secondary schools typically start in what would be the US equivalent of tenth grade (age sixteen) and go on for three years (four for highly technical fields like engineering or computer science). Graduates come away with the kind of technical skills one would gain in a rigorous community college associate's degree program, but with a significant addition. Strong vocational programs combine school and work in the chosen career area, so "career ready" in these countries means that young people have already had three years of experience in a company when they move into the labor market at their apprenticeship firm or elsewhere.

In 2013, we had the privilege of visiting the Swiss Vocational Education and Training system, known as VET, with leaders from the Pathways Network, and saw a system in which 70 percent of young people at age fifteen chose the upper-secondary vocational path rather than an academic path. We saw a system that was able to serve young people from a wide range of backgrounds and with a wide range of academic abilities and that enjoyed broad support from parents, employers, and policy makers. We talked with young people who were not at all embarrassed to say that they had no patience for sitting in school all day, and could explain why they strongly preferred the mix of school and work that brings them a stipend (between $800 and $1,200 a month), makes them feel grown up, and gives them a window into their adult futures. And we saw a system with a youth unemployment rate of under 5 percent even during the fiscal crisis, and upper-secondary completion rates of over 90 percent. We also saw a system in which employers welcomed young people who brought fresh ideas, great questions, energy, and talent into the workplace.

The Swiss system, especially its employers, treats teens as budding adults with contributions to make in the adult world of careers, an attitude quite different from what we are accustomed to at home. Seeing young people at work in a variety of settings in Switzerland—factories, banks, insurance agencies, automotive shops, nursing homes, and IT companies—convinced the Pathways team that choosing a broad first career area at age fifteen is a positive step, not a limiting one. And it is one that aids the maturing process rather than truncating it. We saw sixteen-year-olds dispensing medications to the elderly, and, in the Swiss railroad system, given enough training and responsibility that they had the power to stop a train (a power which they told us proudly they would of course use only in an emergency). Trainers and teachers in Switzerland have the attitude that, naturally, people change careers; once a plumber or a web designer does not mean always. The goal is to give each young person enough work experience to launch them into a first career, open the door to postsecondary education, and ensure that they become lifelong learners.

DESIGNING THE GRADE 9–14 APPROACH IN THE UNITED STATES: CTE AND BEYOND

We knew from the outset that while elements of the European system could be adapted here, we had to work with US building blocks and create a design suited to the United States. We did not begin with the reform or modernization of career and technical education, although that is a worthy goal, given that only about one in four high school students today earns three CTE credits or more. Many CTE students are already being introduced to the work world, an experience that gives school a purpose and often starts these young people on a first career. Indeed, CTE students have higher high school completion rates and higher college entrance rates than students who do not participate.[2]

The reason we use the term "career-focused education" is because we believe all students need exposure to the world of work, not just the fraction who spend significant time in vocational courses. But given that work preparation is seen as the purview of CTE, one challenge is to ensure that our approach does not become narrowly defined to include only programs that meet the federal CTE guidelines, but is understood to mean something broader.

The Pathways to Prosperity Network often emphasizes STEM content both to avoid the stigma associated with studying the traditional trades alone, and, more positively, to signal that career-focused education entails rigorous math and science now needed in high-paying STEM careers, and that some form of career-focused education is of value to all high school students. In states where there is a bifurcation between CTE schools and academic high schools, it is especially important to talk about career-focused education to signal that academic-focused schools, too, should pay attention to their students' career interests and experiences.

Across the country, access to CTE varies. The main models include:

- state systems with standalone full-time vocational schools and full-time "academic" high schools with little to no CTE or career focus;
- state systems with comprehensive high schools that include CTE;
- state systems with part-time CTE programs, usually standalone and regional, to which students travel from their sending high school; and
- state systems that have a mix of models.

Whatever the state structure, each model has a different starting place in implementing career-focused pathways, and each has room for improvement. However, while a good number have revamped their pathways to be current with regional labor market demand, only the CTE schools and programs typically have substantial work-based learning opportunities available to all students desiring them.

BUILDING BLOCKS

In addition to building from existing CTE systems, our grade 9–14 pathways are based on a strong foundation of three preexisting major secondary and postsecondary reform and improvement initiatives: early college high schools, career academies, and the community college movement toward "guided pathways." Here, we first describe the origins and outcomes of early college. We then discuss the San Francisco–based James Irvine Foundation's Linked Learning initiative, which unified and built upon the many existing

NAF and California Partnership Academies. Similar in design, NAF academies, Partnership Academies, and the Linked Learning approach combine academic and career and technical curricula, provide strong student supports, and offer workplace opportunities through partnership with local employers. Finally, we turn to the reforms taking place in the community college world, where, parallel to career-focused education in high school, structures and approaches are being put in place that include renewed attention to workforce development, further spurred by governors, legislatures, and the business community.

The Early College High School Model

In 2002, the Bill & Melinda Gates Foundation was already deeply engaged in supporting the restructuring of large urban high schools into small autonomous schools, using a variety of models. The Foundation had taken note of two very different schools that combined high school and college: Simon's Rock of Bard College, a school designed for accelerating eleventh and twelfth graders ready to begin college-level work, and Middle College High School at LaGuardia Community College, where students at risk of dropping out of high school were housed on a college campus and put in an educational environment that built their academic skills and persistence through to high school graduation. From these ideas, JFF, with funding from the Gates Foundation, worked with a number of statewide and national intermediary organizations to develop what came to be called "early college high schools."

Early college high schools typically start in ninth grade, operate in partnership with a higher education institution (usually a community college), serve predominately low-income and youth of color, and are designed so that students at risk of not attaining a postsecondary credential can graduate from high school in four or five years with an associate's degree. In other words, the model replaces some high school courses with college courses, putting students on an accelerated path through postsecondary programs. The initial early college high school goal was to increase both high school and four-year college completion rates of low-income students and students of color.

By 2012–13, the last school year for which JFF and evaluators collected data, there were about 280 such schools in the original Gates-sponsored network, serving roughly eighty thousand students, and many more versions of early colleges put in place by states and districts. The original cohorts achieved impressive results. The schools, largely standalone or redesigned small schools, have been extremely successful with a challenging population.

A representative sample of thousands of students in one hundred early colleges showed a 90 percent high school graduation rate, twelve points higher than the national average of 78 percent at that time. Early college students on average graduated with thirty-eight college credits, and roughly 30 percent earned an associate's degree or a postsecondary occupational certificate.[3] All the original early college schools agreed to:

- serve students underrepresented in higher education;
- be supported by a local school district, a higher education institution, and a community;
- integrate high school and college, enabling students to earn one to two years of transferable college credit at no cost to their families;
- include comprehensive academic and social supports; and
- advocate for supportive state-level policies.

Early college high schools were most deeply influential in the grade 9–14 pathways design because they most closely approximated European vocational upper-secondary age and grade spans, and because we could use the substantial research and evaluation on early college high schools to build confidence among US adopters that the foundational building block of Pathways would improve both high school graduation rates and college outcomes. But early colleges as initially imagined by the Gates Foundation and supported by JFF and partner organizations were intended to boost four-year college-going rates with little attention to career choice. In designing grade 9–14 pathways, we reasoned that early college would become even more attractive to young people and their families if career experience and work-based learning were infused. To support this line of thinking, we had positive outcomes from strong CTE high schools and programs, from career academies, and from examples in affluent communities. We often explain the design by saying that grade 9–14 career-focused pathways combine early college high schools' provision of college courses in high school with the integration of academic and technical education found in the best career academies, CTE programs, and vocational schools.

Linked Learning

As noted earlier, the United States had a number of CTE reform and improvement organizations, networks, and school models. The Linked Learning approach differed in that it was intended as a way to reform all high schools in the districts that Irvine funded with the goal of creating wall-to-wall career academies. The "all students" goal was the inspiration of Anne Stanton, who joined the James Irvine Foundation in 2006 as director of youth programs. Stanton arrived at the foundation with a bias from directing a Bay Area nonprofit serving homeless and runaway youth. The young people Stanton worked with all wanted, more than anything, entrée into the labor market. Stanton knew that vocational education had had a troubled history. The perception, especially in communities of color, was that too often vocational programs were "dumping grounds," places to assign students who were deemed not capable of doing the kind of rigorous academic work required for college.

The Linked Learning approach championed by the Irvine Foundation differed in two major ways from the design dimensions of Pathways to Prosperity. First, despite the dismal completion statistics for four-year colleges, they advocated for four-year "college for all"; in practice, that meant that all California young people should complete preparation for admission to the University of California and the California State University systems. Community colleges barely figured except as transfer vehicles in their original design. Second, while the Linked Learning approach advocated for college completion, early college or dual enrollment did not figure in the design. The aspiration was that young people graduating from a Linked Learning high school would be well prepared for college; they would succeed because they had career experience and aspirations and the academic strengths and motivation needed.

To its credit, however, Irvine was the first national foundation to step up to the challenge of providing career-focused education for all. A decade later, other private foundations and corporate philanthropies are just beginning to show interest and, of course, this is the model embraced by the Pathways to Prosperity states. As with early college high schools, the Linked Learning or career academy approach has been modified and embraced by new players.[4] In 2014, the California career academy movement received a major boost through the enactment of the California Career Pathways Trust (profiled in chapter 7), a $500 million competitive grants program akin to Linked Learning in integrating career and academic approaches in the high school years, but also requiring both employer and postsecondary collaboration.

No community in California was better positioned to capitalize on the state's massive investment in career pathways than Long Beach. It had long been a poster child for Linked Learning, with its large high schools all organized into wall-to-wall academies, but it also was known throughout the state for the Long Beach Promise, a seamless pathway enabling young people to progress more easily from the Long Beach Unified School District to Long Beach City College and to California State University, Long Beach. Long Beach won two awards totaling $21 million in the first round of the Career Pathways Trust competition, and it has led the way in demonstrating how the principles of Linked Learning can be extended into a career pathways model.

Community Colleges and Guided Pathways

Several trends in the current decade of community college reform support better outcomes for all students—young or older—and are very much in keeping with the Pathways approach. Many community colleges have stepped up to the task of serving young people who seek a leg up into the labor market. Despite limited or even decreasing state support, community colleges have improved the quality, array, and accessibility of their career or CTE pathways, the two-year degrees that prepared students to enter the labor market. Many majors and certificate programs are being revamped to better serve as engines of workforce preparation. In addition, particularly in systems established mainly to prepare students for transfer, community colleges are pivoting to refine and improve career-focused programs, and to ensure that even a career-focused degree has sufficient rigor and breadth that students don't lose credits when they reenter higher education after a stint in the labor market. In 2017, the process of refining and improving career-focused programs continues apace and is serving Pathways to Prosperity and other initiatives focused on supporting students to move into high-demand areas of the economy with decent wages and opportunities to advance.

There is now a strong evidence base, for example, that tells us students do much better when counseled into a default or "guided" pathway with a structured schedule rather than being left with little support to choose among a bewildering array of courses. Guided pathways are an antidote to the traditional "cafeteria" model curriculum, where choice is touted and routes to completion are unclear. Historically, the underlying assumption behind the cafeteria model was that more choice meant greater satisfaction, when in fact too many choices can be overwhelming and lead to poor decisions.[5] In relation to low-income students who often have very complicated and demanding lives beyond the classroom, a plethora of choices often leads to too rapid and uninformed decisions, and ultimately a waste of time and money. Wrong choices also take a toll on motivation to succeed.[6] The Community College Research Center's 2015 research shows a correlation between students who enter a community college program of study early (meaning they take three courses in their chosen program) and higher completion rates.[7]

Thus, the community college field has come to coalesce around the underlying idea that colleges should require students to sign on to a roadmap, and this has become "best practice." Community colleges are developing program outlines that show students just what they will need to do to complete a degree, and at best, guaranteeing that the courses in the guided pathway will be available to those students as planned.[8] An additional trend that is consistent with the grade 9–14 pathways approach is that community colleges are increasingly taking the view—a long time in coming—that all students, whether transferring or completing a two-year degree or certification, are in college to prepare for a career, and therefore the academic versus CTE divide should end. This is certainly the view of employers who continue to assert in polls and surveys that broad so-called liberal arts courses are as critical as technical or career-focused knowledge and skills.

As the Pathways Network evolved, the movement to implement guided pathways in the nation's community colleges was as fortuitous as the development of an evidence base that early college "works." Today, entry into a guided career pathway generally begins once a student completes remediation. But when a community college asks a student to plan backward from a career goal to create his or her own guided pathway, it is not such a stretch to create pathways starting in ninth grade. This is what the many community colleges and high schools in the Pathways Network are doing. Planning backward in this way requires close collaboration across differing education sectors. In early college career-focused high schools, students begin their college-level work earlier and accelerate degree attainment, an approach requiring not only a guided pathway, but one in which courses are aligned across high school and higher education. The alignment process is discussed in chapter 3.

THE PATHWAYS FRAMEWORK AND IMPLEMENTATION LEVERS

The economic recovery was still in doubt when we began our work with the initial five states in 2012. With unemployment rising, states disinvesting in public higher education (which caused tuition to go up), and the job market for young people shrinking dramatically, access to work became part of the national conversation. Two opposing trends heightened interest in career pathways: unemployment and underemployment increased, even among young people with degrees, and simultaneously, the number of people entering college grew. Economic data made clear that those suffering the greatest labor market difficulties were young people just entering the workforce during the crisis, especially those who had only a high school diploma or had chosen a postsecondary credential unwisely.

To combat this, we envisioned statewide systems of grade 9–14 pathways with the goal of propelling all students to earn not only diplomas, but also career-focused postsecondary credentials of high value to regional employers in high-growth, high-demand fields. By the latter, we mean a college degree that provides sufficient technical and general knowledge in a career area that students can enter the labor market immediately. However, students should be able to earn a good enough salary to enable them to continue their education in the future should they choose to do so. Under the best circumstances, their employer will provide tuition benefits for further education, and they will be able to proceed with clear goals. By statewide "systems," we mean that career pathways are the default organizing structure that regions and states use to align high schools and community colleges, whether the goal is transfer or entry into the labor market.

All of the building blocks described here led us to develop a simple framework organized around five implementation "levers" in order to guide the work of Pathways Network members. The five levers are grade 9–14 pathways; career awareness, exposure, and work-based learning; employer engagement; intermediaries; and policy (see table 2.1). These simple levers have served the Network well as high-level guidance to implementers and policy makers, leaving ample room for local, regional, and state Pathways leaders to design their systems with sensitivity to their unique conditions.

In the next chapter, we profile some of our leading states and regions to show how the framework and levers apply to the work happening on the ground.

TABLE 2.1   Pathways to Prosperity Framework

Levers for implementation	What the work looks like
Grade 9–14 pathways	High schools and community colleges create career pathways in grades 9–14, with clear structures, timelines, costs, and requirements, that link and integrate high school and postsecondary curricula and align both levels of education with labor market needs.
Career awareness, exposure, and work-based learning	Starting in the middle grades, students are exposed to a wide range of career options, information, and opportunities to learn about high school and postsecondary courses of study leading to careers. Students engage in a grade 9–14 continuum of work-based learning opportunities in their chosen career areas. Intermediaries, employers, and community-based organizations help young people make informed choices throughout each grade 9–14 pathway.
Employer engagement	Employers commit to providing a continuum of learning opportunities at the workplace throughout the grade 9–14 pathway. Employers collaborate with educators and are supported by intermediaries in structuring and managing workplace learning. Employers support students' transitions into the local labor market.
Intermediaries	Local or regional intermediaries serve as conveners, brokers, and technical assistance providers to schools and employers engaged in building and sustaining pathways. Intermediaries recruit business, nonprofit, and public employers and ensure that participating leaders understand and support the vision.
Policy	State dual enrollment policies provide access for low-income students. Districts and community colleges have financial incentives and sustainable funding to provide grade 9–14 programs of study in career and technical education and leading to diplomas, certificates, or associate's degrees. Accountability systems weight dual enrollment courses as they weight Advanced Placement (AP) and International Baccalaureate (IB) courses. The state provides incentives for employers and unions to offer work experience opportunities.

CHAPTER 3

HOW IT LOOKS
ON THE GROUND

The first Pathways states joined the network because leaders wanted to respond to the educational needs and requirements of the still-forgotten half, those young people who arrive in their mid-twenties without a useable credential. Among the key observations in the *Pathways* report, one that caught readers' attention and seemed to surprise them was that other countries were doing much better by their young people than the United States, especially in preparing youth for the work world. As noted in prior chapters, the difference was that other countries had vocational education *systems* that were attractive to a wide range of students, provided substantial flexibility and choice, and resulted in smooth transitions into the labor market. The results were very low rates of youth unemployment and a set of highly skilled young people. While these systems could not simply be duplicated in the United States, they have provided powerful illustrations of a range of options that might be possible to implement.

The European example helped states to name the problem: to promote healthy and successful youth development, schools needed to provide many more young people with knowledge about careers, preparation for them, and experience in work sites. And most school systems did not have a system for doing so. The *Pathways* report led states to turn to their own CTE programs to examine practices that could be spread and lessons about school design and culture that could be leveraged; in the results of CTE programs, states saw higher high school graduation rates, greater engagement, and a sense of purposefulness lacking in mainstream high school programs.

Illustrations of what could be accomplished with a wide range of students came from exemplary CTE programs, particularly in the southern states, where students move freely between CTE and other discipline-based courses within one building. In the rural South—where high schools are regional—school districts are county-wide, and greater numbers of students have historically entered the workforce after high school rather than going on to college. A good number of such programs have internships built in, and have strong employer engagement. What they were missing was a postsecondary connection.

Many urban centers also have exemplary career-focused education. For example, New York City has over fifty CTE or career-themed high schools. Some are small early colleges with strong corporate partners; others are well-established large schools focused on aviation, health care, or a range of technical occupations like engineering and biotech. The problem in the United States is not a lack of examples of high-quality CTE or other career-focused programs. Rather, what has been missing is examples of states or large regions with *systems* in place designed to equip most students with the skills, credentials, and work experience necessary to make a successful transition into today's more challenging labor market.

In this chapter, we provide a set of profiles illustrating how a mix of model state and regional Network members have used the Pathways framework to design and build systems that can enable many more young people to make the kind of successful transition from the end of compulsory schooling into working life that we have seen in higher performing systems abroad.

The strategies that these states and regions have chosen to pursue around grade 9–14 pathway development vary, as does the degree to which we can attribute progress or lack thereof to guidance and technical assistance from the Pathways to Prosperity team. Some states had a head start in that they already had widespread CTE programs. Others signed on because they recognized that, while they once had had substantial career-focused programs, in the last decade, attention to careers was eclipsed by pressure to raise test scores in the core academic subjects in order to meet the requirements of state high school accountability systems. Factors that differentiate speed, depth, and quality of career pathway implementation include:

- status of pathways on the ground at Pathways launch;
- leadership, whether an organization or visible champion;
- initial ambition for scale; and
- whether the work is centralized and primarily top down, demand-driven from the ground up, or some combination of both.

GETTING STARTED

Once a state joins the Pathways to Prosperity Network, the first step is for the state to designate one or two economic regions where state leaders feel there are sufficient assets already in place—strong secondary or postsecondary CTE programs, motivated employers concerned about their future workforce needs, respected intermediary organizations—to introduce the career pathways approach. The Pathways team then works with state leaders to design and implement an asset mapping process. This is typically a two- or three-day exercise in which a JFF team interviews seventy-five to one hundred regional stakeholders using the Pathways framework to develop an understanding of the region's strengths and gaps.

We have carried out the process in more than sixty diverse regions where Network initiatives are located. We use the levers of the Pathways framework as a guide, and provide stakeholders with feedback on the strengths in their regions as well as where they will need particular effort for each lever (see chapter 2 for more on the framework and levers). The purposes of asset mapping are:

- to assemble baseline data about the region in relation to the five levers of the Pathways framework to determine a starting point for planning;
- within the limits of a short visit, to bring a helpful "outsider" look to the region from a national perspective;
- to serve as the foundation for the twelve- to eighteen-month work plan to be written by local leaders; and

- to help identify other stakeholders with the energy and commitment to come together with regional leaders to help drive system reform.

From the twenty- to forty-page asset mapping reports, rich with data and observations, recommendations emerge. Pathways team members present the findings and recommendations to the lead stakeholders, and usually to the broader concerned community. A labor market analysis consistently identifies similar labor market growth areas across the Network's states as the best bets for young people seeking entry-level jobs with a two-year degree. These typically are health care, IT, and advanced manufacturing. In addition, in some locales, agriculture, financial services, and transportation, distribution, and logistics (TDL) also emerge. In the latter field, we are careful to distinguish between jobs such as truck driver or warehouse worker—which are low-wage, lack a career ladder, and are not appropriate for a young person—and roles that can lead to technical or management careers with good wages. Construction also often emerges as a rebounding industry.

The asset mapping report provides the basis for regional leaders to develop a work plan to guide the development of their regional grade 9–14 pathways strategy. These regional work plans, which are constantly being revised and updated, then serve to guide the advice and assistance provided by the Pathways team to the state and region. See the sidebars on pages 43 and 44 for excerpts from asset mapping carried out in Minnesota's Greater Twin Cities in fall 2015 and in East Tennessee in late spring 2015.

The schools, districts, and community colleges described are representative of what we have found in urban, suburban, and rural areas among state systems. High schools generally have a starting place for career pathways, so Pathways to Prosperity can be introduced not as a new initiative, but as a way to build from the foundation to expand opportunities to a larger group of students. That is, even if the academic high school does not have a CTE program, the district or region certainly will have one.

On the postsecondary side, even if the community college partner has a substantial history of dual enrollment of high school students, few postsecondary institutions have backmapped programs of study in their career

Representative Asset Mapping Findings:
Two Minnesota Districts

The Twin Cities lead is our partner and funder, Greater Twin Cities United Way, one of the strongest and most experienced intermediaries among the Pathways members. Districts participating in the initiative include Minneapolis Public Schools, St. Paul Public Schools, White Bear Lake Area Schools, Bloomington Public Schools, and Burnsville Public Schools. Across the initiative, students are currently enrolled in thirteen career academies and eight more are expected to open in fall 2017. The stakeholders' goal is to enroll 650 students annually by 2017 and 2,200 students annually by 2024.

St. Paul Public Schools hosts two NAF academies, a small Academy of Finance at Como Park Senior High School (graduation rate: 75 percent) and an Academy of IT at Humboldt High School (graduation rate: 79 percent). A US Department of Labor Employment & Training Administration Youth CareerConnect grant provides additional funding for the NAF academies. The IT pathway is strong and aligns well with the key components for a career academy. Coursework is clearly aligned to college credentials, and the course sequence includes multiple opportunities for earning college credit. Student learning outcomes, coursework, and student work are aligned to a robust work-based learning continuum. Right Track and HIRED provide work-based learning opportunities to students in the district. About fifty to seventy-five students in the district participate in concurrent enrollment.

The Pathways work is ramping up in the White Bear Lake Area High School (graduation rate: 96 percent), particularly in manufacturing. The district sits "on a bed of manufacturing partners," and thus the first pathway is in manufacturing/engineering. Partners include a host of employers, Hennepin Technical College, HIRED, and the Vadnais Heights Economic Development Corporation. The district hopes to prepare students for a variety of postsecondary options that lead toward a variety of credentials, including National Institute for Metalworking Skills (NIMS) certification. There is ongoing work to align high school pathways to programs of study at the local community college as well as advanced coursework, including AP, Project Lead the Way, College in the Schools with the University of Minnesota, and concurrent enrollment with Century College.

Source: Jobs for the Future, Twin Cities Asset Mapping Project: A Pathways to Prosperity Network Report (Boston: JFF, 2016).

Representative Asset Mapping Findings:
Two East Tennessee Counties

The East Tennessee region comprises fifteen counties. Knox County is the most populous, with 434,000 residents, or over one-third of the region's total population. The Knox County Career Magnet Academy (CMA) serves as an example of what other schools might become. Hamblen County is more rural, but like other areas in Tennessee it is host to small and medium manufacturers, a number with headquarters in Japan and Germany, that make auto parts for the larger manufacturers in the South.

In fall 2014, CMA, a Title I school, launched four pathways: sustainable agriculture, homeland security, advanced manufacturing, and teacher preparation. Project-based learning, service learning, and work-based learning are integrated into the pathways curriculum. Students also have extensive opportunities to learn about careers, with time set aside one day per week for career exploration activities, and CMA has in place curricula focused on college and career readiness and employability skills. The school has also developed a teacher externship program. CMA students begin taking dual-credit courses at the college starting in ninth grade; students have the opportunity to fully dually enroll at the college during their junior year. CMA is located on the campus of Pellissippi State Community College at Strawberry Plains. The Knoxville Chamber of Commerce is working with CMA to identify and recruit employer partners.

Leaders in the Hamblen County Schools are working to align the district's CTE offerings with both labor market demand and with available programs of study at Tennessee Colleges of Applied Technology–Morristown. Currently, 45 percent of students in the district are enrolled in seven pathways, but district leaders would like to scale up pathways to enroll 100 percent of students. Across the region, several challenges exist to implementing pathways. Currently, academic and CTE courses are distinct from one another. Because teacher salaries are much lower than those in industry, it is difficult for districts to find the teachers they would need to create pathways aligned with labor market demand. Finally, as in all rural areas, transportation is a challenge that will need to be taken on as part of the Pathways work.

Source: Jobs for the Future, East Tennessee Asset Mapping Project: A Pathways to Prosperity Network Report (Boston: JFF, 2015).

majors to align with high school curricula leading to career credentials. The community colleges, while eager to partner, are just at the beginning of this work.

FLEXIBILITY AND ADAPTABILITY OF THE NETWORK

In subsequent chapters, we will provide more detail about how each lever in the Pathways framework plays out on the ground. For now, however, we want to make two more general observations about how we approach the work with our members. First, we believe that a big piece of our value-add is the Pathways framework itself in that it can enable a state or region to bring together what is often a bewildering number of disconnected, overlapping initiatives into a cohesive plan of action. We work hard to ensure that Pathways to Prosperity does not become yet another initiative layered on top of existing initiatives but rather a vehicle for coordinating and making more coherent what already exists and identifying the priorities for the next level of work.

Our second observation has to do with the interplay between states and regions. Although we set up the Network initially as a consortium of states, we understood from the beginning that the work of building career pathways systems plays out primarily at the regional labor market level. In a large, complex state like California, it is obvious that regions like Silicon Valley, the Central Valley, and the East Bay have distinctive economies that require distinctive career pathways, but even tiny Delaware with only three counties has regional labor market variation. With the importance of regions in mind, we have several regions that joined the Network without their states. In the second year of the Network, the metropolitan Columbus area, a major region in Ohio, asked to become a member without its state; the next year two more regions, metro Madison (Wisconsin) and the Greater Twin Cities (Minnesota), joined as well.

While our preference remains to work with states and their regions because of the policy levers that the states control, it is the regional work that is really at the center of our Pathways strategy. That said, our three metro regional members are in regular communication with their state agencies because their work cannot help but be affected by the state policy and regulatory environment. One new development at the end of 2016 was the decision of leaders in two major urban centers with expansive regional labor markets, New York City and Philadelphia, to join the Network. Both are the major cities of their states and serve as laboratories for state policies, whether barriers or supports.

SPOTLIGHT: PATHWAYS TO PROSPERITY STATES

Two states, Tennessee and Delaware, are promising success stories in the Pathways Network. They have carried out statewide asset mapping over the last several years, provide all schools and their partner colleges with technical assistance, and are thus the most advanced among the Pathways states in developing grade 9–14 pathway systems.

Like all states, they previously had CTE programs for high school students, but course content needed to be upgraded and modernized, and few career-focused pathways included dual enrollment and reached into community college. In the years leading up to Pathways membership, both states had been more focused on improving traditional academic outcomes, especially in math and English, than they had been on CTE. In fact, these states' single-minded commitment to improving academic achievement had been confirmed in 2009 when they became the first two states funded in the highly competitive federal Race to the Top initiative.[1]

To begin Pathways development, the governors in each state used their bully pulpit to initiate and publicize the need for a career pathways approach. Each formed cross-sector leadership groups representing labor, education, and employment to guide and champion the work. In Tennessee, Pathways rode the coattails of Governor Bill Haslam's Drive to 55 initiative, setting the goal of raising from 32 to 55 the percentage of Tennesseans with a college degree or certificate by 2025. This was followed in 2014 by the governor's Tennessee Promise, his highly publicized free technical and community college tuition plan, the first of its kind in the nation. In January 2015, following on the heels of Governor Haslam, Delaware Governor Jack Markell announced the Delaware Promise, which established a vision for education and workforce development and set a goal that 65 percent of the state's workforce would earn a college degree or professional certificate, and every high school student would graduate college and career ready by 2025.

Both states took a systemic approach, starting not with pilots but with a strategy focused on building capacity to address all five levers of the Pathways framework. Both states had strong leadership from the top, political leadership from the governor, and implementation leadership from the state education agency, but both were also committed to building on the good work already going on in the field. While the challenges are very different in the two states—one with fewer than a million citizens, only one community college, 32 regular high schools, and 6 CTE schools; the other with a population of 6.5 million, 336 high schools, and 10 standalone CTE schools—both have now moved to scale. All nine economic regions of Tennessee are now in play, and in Delaware—where the whole state is the size of one Tennessee region—six thousand total students are in pathways across all high schools, and a growing number are linked through dual enrollment with Delaware Technical Community College. We provide more detail on each state here.

Tennessee

Five years into Pathways building, Tennessee has refined state policies needed to support a pathways system. The initiative, called Pathways Tennessee, has benefited tremendously from the creation of a very active cross-agency leadership team that works collaboratively to transform the state's career preparation system.

The JFF Pathways team has now carried out asset mapping in each of the Tennessee economic regions, identified intermediaries and defined their roles, and helped mobilize employers around the Pathways agenda. Tennessee hired staff to support regions, and made grants to intermediaries from federal Perkins Reserve funds to spark innovation. Tennessee high schools are becoming vertically aligned with their region's TCATs—the Tennessee

Colleges of Applied Technology. These schools, which have long provided short-term state-of-the-art technical and professional training for adults, are now aligning with high school technical programs and attuning themselves to the needs of younger students.

Over the last decade, Tennessee has greatly expanded dual enrollment participation by providing districts and postsecondary institutions with sample memoranda of understanding (MOU), creating funding paths to pay for advanced coursework, and enabling dual enrollment and dual credit policy to better serve the students and educational institutions. All Tennessee juniors and seniors are eligible to access up to $1,200 per year through the Tennessee Dual Enrollment Grant, funded by the Tennessee Lottery and administered by the Tennessee Student Assistance Corporation. Students in Tennessee can also remain on their high school campus to take dual credit courses, which allow students to earn both academic and technical credit hours toward their high school graduation requirements while simultaneously earning credits that are accepted across a number of postsecondary institutions, once students enroll post-graduation. Tennessee Transfer Pathways is a systemic agreement across some public postsecondary institutions allowing for student dual enrollment credits to apply toward higher-level credentials, certifications, and/or degrees. But at this writing, strong and popular CTE programs in high schools are only beginning to build dual enrollment programs of study through the associate's degree at the state's thirteen community colleges.[2]

An example of a strong high school CTE program is Cookeville High School, in Upper Cumberland, Tennessee, an early regional member of Pathways. Cookeville High has a representative array of CTE programs in a high school serving a broad geographic area. Cookeville High School serves twenty-two hundred students in a rural region spanning 408 square miles. While there are three high schools in the county, Cookeville High serves as the vocational education hub for all three.[3] Programs include advanced manufacturing, agriculture, business, computer programming, cosmetology, family consumer science, engineering, and web design.[4] Many of these programs are strong, with up-to-date equipment and instructors who are current with their fields. Cookeville is a step ahead of many Tennessee high schools in that it hosts a postsecondary mechatronics lab sponsored by one of Tennessee's well-regarded TCATs. In a visit to the TCAT wing of the high school, we were impressed by the diversity of the students, whose plans ranged from entering the labor force with their postsecondary mechatronics credential to attaining a graduate engineering degree. In addition, both Tennessee Technological University and Volunteer State Community College offer a range of career-focused dual enrollment courses at the Cookeville Higher Education Campus.

While most high schools are not this far along, all Tennessee high school students are benefiting from a number of initiatives intended to better prepare them for postsecondary education and to lower remediation rates. These include the Tennessee Promise, mentioned earlier, which nudges applicants into research-based behaviors known to increase college preparation and retention. To attain the promised last-dollar scholarship, students must apply early in their senior year, complete the Free Application for Federal Student Aid (FAFSA), attend mandatory advising sessions prior to beginning school, attend college full-time, and meet virtually or in person with mentors a prescribed number of times per year. A second initiative, SAILS (Seamless Alignment and Integrated Learning Support), embeds developmental education competencies into high school senior year math and English courses, utilizing a blended learning model so that students begin college with credit-bearing courses.[5] And finally, Tennessee is getting positive results from scaling a corequisite approach to math, reading, and writing in its thirteen community colleges.[6]

Delaware

Because of its size, the Delaware Pathways initiative was able to see changes on the ground quickly. In 2014 Governor Markell convened a state leadership team that has driven the Delaware Pathways work over the last three years. The Delaware Pathways initiative has supported the development of regional CTE pathways that accelerate academic and technical instruction, are responsive to labor market demand, and engage employers. These pathways are now being scaled across the state in high-demand industry sectors like finance, health care, culinary and hospitality management, computer science and networking, manufacturing, and logistics and production, as well as in science and engineering. Each pathway offers high school students the opportunity to earn an industry-recognized credential, early college credit, and relevant work experience.

The Delaware Department of Education and its partners have developed ten demand-driven state-model CTE career pathways, which are available for consideration and adoption by districts. These regional career pathways began in the 2015–16 and 2016–17 school years. Three additional career pathways were released for school district consideration in September 2016 and launch in the 2017–18 school year. For each state-model CTE career pathway, the Department has made available an analysis of labor market information on its website in order to inform adoption decisions made by school district leaders.[7] Delaware Technical Community College is similarly committed to the use of labor market information to drive program design, and its career pathways are aligned with high-demand sectors of Delaware's economy.[8]

Delaware has created a set of model CTE programs of study, each mapped to a demand-driven occupation, with a defined course sequence and instructional outline, opportunities for students to earn college credit and an industry-recognized credential, support for school administrators and counselors, and course-specific professional learning opportunities for teachers. Further, all state-model CTE programs of study are developed in conjunction with representatives from business and industry, secondary and postsecondary educators, and community stakeholders.[9]

The Delaware Pathways leadership team anticipates that pathways will be in place in all school districts in the state by the 2017–2018 school year. In 2015–16, Delaware Pathways served 5 percent of the state's high school students. In 2016–17, that percentage has increased to 15 percent. The 2019 goal is to have 50 percent of high school students (twenty thousand) complete a career pathway. To facilitate that goal, the state is expanding dual enrollment, with a 2019 target of six thousand slots, but if the state wants to ramp up the percentage of students who complete at least twelve college credits in high school, they may need to expand dual enrollment and rethink the cost to students.

SPOTLIGHT: PATHWAYS TO PROSPERITY REGIONS

Here we profile the system-building work under way in three promising Network regions. We chose these regional sites to exemplify different stages and approaches to building grade 9–14 pathways:

- Central Ohio has made a strong start in designing a career pathways system anchored in a community college that serves students throughout the region and as a hub for pathways.
- In Marlborough, Massachusetts, we focus on an ambitious STEM early college career pathways system under development in a single suburban district, partnering with a regional workforce board, two regional higher education institutions, and a set of high-tech employers that will anchor a broader regional strategy. This is one of three sites in the state that are participating in a federally funded Youth CareerConnect project coordinated by the JFF Pathways team.
- In the Central Valley of California, we profile the best example in our Network of an employer-led initiative, the Wonderful Company's Agriculture Prep program. This commitment of a major regional employer improves the life chances of young people in a highly impoverished rural area.

All three regions have received competitive federal, state, and/or philanthropic grant funding to build out and expand pathways development using the Pathways framework. Grant sources include Ohio's Straight A Fund initiative and the Joyce Foundation; federal Youth CareerConnect and i3 programs; and California's Career Pathways Trust, all providing substantial multiyear support.

Central Ohio

Since 2011, Columbus State Community College has led a regional strategy, the Central Ohio Compact, to build a better-prepared talent pipeline for the regional economy. Operating through Columbus State Community College, the Compact facilitates regional collaboration and communication across forty-three school districts, eleven college and university partners, fifteen public-sector partners, and ten industry partners. The Compact also works closely with the region's chambers of commerce and has existing educational relationships with area businesses. It has a data dashboard that integrates K–12, postsecondary, and workforce data on outcomes and assists both educational institutions and area businesses with information on regional progress toward the 60 percent postsecondary credential goal by 2025, adopted from the Lumina Foundation's national goal.

With support from JPMorgan Chase, the Ohio Business Roundtable, Battelle Memorial Institute, and the Educational Service Center serving twenty-eight districts within six counties of Central Ohio, the Compact adopted goals to increase both degree completion and workforce preparation. In 2013, Governor John Kasich and the Ohio legislature created the Straight A Fund, a $250 million fund to award competitive grants designed to reduce the cost of education and create innovative and sustainable programs that improve educational outcomes across the state. Using the Pathways to Prosperity framework as a guide, a coalition of districts led by Reynoldsburg Public Schools in partnership with Columbus State applied for consortium funding and received $14 million through the Straight A Fund for the formation of regional in-demand career pathways; the region was awarded a second grant of $8.8 million in 2014 to assist with data related to pathways.

In 2015, with JFF, Columbus State won two more substantial grants: an i3 grant of $11.5 million from the US Department of Education, and a smaller grant of $400,000 from the Joyce Foundation to join the Great Lakes College and Career Pathways Initiative—a peer-learning community across three states and four regions. Other related funding includes a $5 million grant from American Electric Power to Columbus City Schools in 2013 for STEM dual enrollment courses at five high schools, and FastPath, a $1.5 million grant from the City of Columbus to spur community collaboration in pathways with Nationwide Children's Hospital. The regional pathways work in Central Ohio is led by a respected former superintendent from a leading district in the consortium, whose title at Columbus State is superintendent of school and community partnerships.

This infusion of funding has not been without challenges—for example, managing initiatives with differing timelines, goals, reporting requirements, and lead staff—although it has certainly advanced the work in a number of sites. The pathways include coursework at the high school and college level in advanced manufacturing, IT, logistics, and health care. Industries were selected based on regional economic need and targeted growth areas. Columbus State assured alignment of courses and course progressions with recognized industry certifications and degree programs.

Since the initiation of Pathways, Columbus State has seen significant growth and movement in three key areas necessary to scaling grade 9–14 career pathways: state dual enrollment policy, digitized course delivery for Compact high schools, and expanded high school–college instructor collaboration. The new state policy, College Credit Plus, requires each high school in the state to provide two college-credit pathway options—one for fifteen credits and one for thirty—at no cost to students.

With the exponential increase in the number of high school partnerships with a single community college and a changed and substantially more open state dual enrollment policy, Columbus State has had to create and continuously improve a system to assess, advise, and place large numbers of high school students in programs of study to ensure their success in completing a degree or certificate. Columbus State negotiated dual enrollment MOUs with many district partners based on the new state policies, including an agreement that it would pay for textbooks for high school students in the first year, a hidden and significant expense of dual enrollment that would otherwise be borne by high schools under College Credit Plus.

The new dual enrollment policy and the Compact goal to accelerate degree attainment impelled Columbus State to improve its course delivery system aimed at high schools. The community college developed digitized courses that pair high school and Columbus State faculty with digitized course content created by the faculty. The faculty member is responsible for all course content and assessment and works closely with the high school teacher, who provides critical on-site support to students who are learning content digitally. Students may be in dedicated high school classes, in Columbus State Community College classes at a regional learning center, in online courses, or on campus, but all have to show up on the roster of Columbus State faculty. To accommodate the increased demand for dual enrollment, Columbus State has had to streamline its processes for registering and orienting high school students and ensuring that they are properly coded for tracking and addressing state compliance requirements.

Digitized courses have been developed that lead to certifications in advanced manufacturing, health care, IT, and logistics. High school teacher credentials to teach dual enrollment courses are approved by the Columbus State faculty. A three-day professional development program provides the opportunity for Columbus State faculty and high school teachers to develop relationships that ensure the effective delivery of the college courses.

Some particularly effective policies and practices include a manufacturing pathway that will be scaled to serve all the schools in the region, using mobile "Fab Labs" with cutting-edge advanced manufacturing/preengineering equipment and machinery in trailers that can be rotated through schools. Project Lead the Way courses in middle and high school lead into a college program of study, followed by two full-time semesters paid by federal work study and full-time job opportunities at the completion of the associate's degree.[10] A major policy change allows high school students in Columbus State's aligned health pathway to directly enter the nursing program after completing the prerequisite courses and meeting the GPA standard. In a first-of-its-kind agreement, two districts are sharing health-related equipment, facilities, and instructors, providing more students with opportunities to earn postsecondary health credentials that lead to a job as well as further education.

Several years into the work, the original Pathways working group of eighteen districts is no longer in place, but Columbus State continues to produce new pathways for high school students. The college's website has extensive access to advising, programs of study, application and orientation processes, and more, and calls out the special pathways available only to Innovation Generation high school students.[11]

Marlborough, Massachusetts

Massachusetts has both a high performing regional vocational system and high performing comprehensive and academic high schools. By choosing an academic or comprehensive high school, eighth graders are limiting their chances for a CTE concentration. Young people in academic high schools in many low- to middle-income rural or suburban Massachusetts communities get little career-focused advising, preparation, or experience. We call out low- to middle-income communities because high schools in the most affluent communities do provide more career-focused educational experiences, often under the banner of internships, service learning, or senior capstone projects. For example, Wellesley High School, in an affluent suburb of Boston (average household income $214,000, median home price $830,000), has no CTE program. However, the high school offers such career-focused courses as TV production, digital art and design, advertising and marketing, and engineering tech and robotics, and senior projects take place at the New England Aquarium, Boston Children's Hospital, and the like.

Yet over the last few years, Massachusetts has begun to develop impressive career pathways work in just the kinds of districts that had none in the past. Here we take a look at a STEM early college high school in a suburb thirty miles west of Boston. With funding from a Massachusetts Department of Elementary and Secondary Education Race to the Top grant and technical assistance from Jobs for the Future, Marlborough launched a STEM early college high school in fall 2011. In 2014, JFF, the Marlborough Public Schools, and the Partnership for a Skilled Workforce—the region's workforce board—applied for a federal Youth CareerConnect grant using the Pathways framework as the guiding rubric.[12] JFF, Marlborough, and two other sites in the state were awarded $4.9 million to scale up innovative high school models geared to regional labor market needs over five years. Beyond

JFF, the work was supported by the Massachusetts Department of Elementary and Secondary Education's College and Career Readiness unit with contributions from the state's community colleges and workforce boards. STEM early college in Marlborough (M-STEM) is in its sixth year of design and implementation.

The program is targeted to average students who might not have postsecondary aspirations, English language learners (14 percent), Latino students (35 percent), and students with disabilities. Nearly half of the participants are eligible for free or reduced-cost lunch. Marlborough's pathways system begins in sixth grade, and progresses through high school with increasing depth of study, workplace experience, and career knowledge-building in STEM. The program immerses six hundred young people, grades 6–12, in advanced interdisciplinary collaborative projects and work-based learning. M-STEM employs a nontracking, nonleveling approach that is entirely honors-based. Students receive instructional supports as they progress through the problem-based advanced curriculum. Both vertical and horizontal teaming, in the form of professional learning communities, are the teaching mode in both the middle school and high school. The scope and quality of project-based learning has increased over time; currently, middle school students complete one project per semester and high school students complete four projects per year.

Starting in tenth grade, students earn college credits through partnerships with Quinsigamond Community College and Framingham State University, two- and four-year public institutions, respectively, both about a half-hour's drive away. M-STEM has MOUs with these colleges for dual enrollment courses. Students participate in college coursework in their high school, take courses online, and participate in college visits to experience the campus environment. M-STEM has also established a blended model for AP classes that includes articulated courses for skills areas (CAD for college credit) and online college courses. This allows students to complete at least one semester of postsecondary study prior to high school graduation.

Fifty percent of eleventh-grade students elected to enroll in M-STEM's pathways for the 2015–16 school year. M-STEM has identified subpathways matched to career clusters that align well with the governor's economic development agenda: engineering and manufacturing, health care and life science, and computer science and IT. These pathways are coupled with individualized learning/development plans (IDPs). Naviance Family Connection software is used with all students starting their freshman year as a college-/career-planning tool that houses the IDP provided by the state.

The district's STEM director leads the Marlborough initiative. He has established a tight-knit, diligent leadership committee made up of school leaders, workforce board staff, and employers who have been deeply involved in the high school—participating in science fairs, hosting student visits at their companies, and running teacher workshops on design thinking. Youth CareerConnect provides ample financial resources to support the work and M-STEM has district support for scaling pathways. The curriculum for each of the pathways is in place and the scope and sequence are clearly delineated. Grant funds have enabled the district to put teachers through training to integrate new content into the curriculum. Teachers receive stipends for training their peers.

A major event attracting the attention of statewide officials is the annual Marlborough High School STEM Early College High Winter Expo, which showcases the students' science and engineering research and brings in the corporate partners who work with students and their teachers. In 2016, the ninth-grade students displayed their 3D capsules and hovercrafts, while the tenth-grade students exhibited the projects they will enter in the February Science Fair. M-STEM is becoming so well known for quality and scale within a medium-size school system that it is attracting myriad visitors from around the country.

As Marlborough works toward the goal of ensuring that all rising seniors participate in work-based experiences in companies, M-STEM students are participating in an extensive range of school-based career preparation activities. Not only is the curriculum sequenced in such a way that students in grades 6–10 gain the foundational skills and knowledge required for advanced work in grades 11 and 12, but industry perspective and participation are woven into students' daily activities at school. More than a dozen industry partners are making important contributions to in-school activities. Marlborough has already integrated work-related exercises and applications throughout the curriculum, and a menu of visits and activities with employers and professional development programs introduces teachers to business processes. Finding the paid internships for juniors and seniors is the next big challenge.

Central Valley of California

The Wonderful Company is a privately held, $4 billion company with major agricultural holdings in the Central Valley of California. It produces the world's largest crop of tree nuts and such highly recognizable brands as Fiji Water, Pom Wonderful, and Wonderful Halos. Starting in 2002, the company began to act on its recognition that, without education leading to economic opportunity, the communities from which its workers were coming could not thrive. The Wonderful Company provided scholarships and health improvement programs, and started a charter school rich in music and the arts. And in 2013, the company took a major step in terms of scale and resources invested in education by starting Wonderful Agriculture Career Prep Academy (Ag Prep). At this writing, the company's philanthropic investments in education—it also has a major philanthropic investment in health care—have reached more than fifty-five thousand Central Valley students across eighty-three schools in twenty-four districts. The company has awarded more than fifteen hundred college scholarships and incentives, as well as thirteen hundred teacher grants. As a vertically integrated company, it has an education team of fifteen, managed by a seasoned senior vice president with deep public school leadership experience.[13]

Ag Prep directly addresses two pillars of the pathways movement: youth preparation for employment and building an employee pipeline to help the regional economy thrive. According to the Wonderful Company's research, in California's Central Valley, youth unemployment stands at 37 percent, yet there are an estimated fifty-eight thousand middle- and high-skill STEM-based agricultural jobs that will open by 2020. With fewer than thirty-six thousand graduates expected to enter the workforce in that timeframe, there will almost certainly be a significant skills gap. Ag Prep was created to prepare young people for those good jobs, rather than have the ambitious and lucky ones leave the region for opportunities elsewhere. Working with seven middle schools, seven high schools, three community colleges, Fresno State University, and several additional employers, the company's education team, Wonderful Education, is expanding early college career pathways. The JFF Pathways team has been involved in documentation, skills mapping (bringing together employees and community college and high school instructors), as well as getting word out about Ag Prep, since it is as close to the ideal that we have seen.

The program prepares the Valley's young people for three career pathways—plant science, agriculture mechanics, and business management—leading to jobs such as irrigation manager, equipment mechanic, and accountant or analyst. The training required for these jobs requires high levels of math and science, as well as a level of technical expertise that was unknown when these students' families began work in the fields. Wonderful Education touches each component of the Pathways framework—from introducing middle schoolers to the world of work in agriculture, to a sequence of work-based learning experiences, to a paid internship leading to a job. We provide more detail on Wonderful's work-based learning continuum of experience in chapter 5. Each step has been carefully thought out, piloted, revised, and documented. Consequently, the model is now at some scale. As of 2016–17, Ag Prep was serving 825 high school freshmen, sophomores, and juniors, and 1,000 middle schoolers, and continuing to grow.

The company characterizes its work as based on a "contract" between students, parents, and schools—all in an effort to create real-world learning experiences that prepare students for the high-tech jobs of the future. Ag Prep offers a rigorous four-year academic program with substantial dual enrollment. High school students take college courses taught by college professors starting the summer before ninth grade, enabling participants to complete their high school academic requirements and earn college credit, so that by the summer after high school graduation, students will have earned their high school diploma and an associate of science degree tuition-free.

Students can then either enter the agriculture workforce with a guaranteed job (starting wages are around $35,000 to $50,000 per year), or they can go to a four-year college and enter as a junior, finishing in half the time and at half the cost.[14]

Most impressive is the experience of young people in Ag Prep classrooms. The Wonderful Company has invested in expert design of project-based learning experiences to introduce challenges in agriculture. Teachers and community college faculty visit the company's plants and central offices in Los Angeles to learn how a modern corporation operates so that they can draw on their own new knowledge in their classrooms. And employees are prepared and trained for student visits so that tours and job shadows are serious and individualized learning experiences with pre- and post-assignments. While the program is just in its third year, and the work is getting increasingly challenging as the first group of students prepares to meet all high school and community college graduation requirements, the results thus far are impressive and speak to the data-driven, results-oriented leadership of the program.

The results for tenth graders during 2015–16 include:

- *Academic progress.* Sophomores grew by about two academic years in reading and math.
- *On track for college degree.* Seventy-five percent are on track for earning their associate of science degree by the summer after high school graduation (they passed five or six college classes by the end of sophomore year).
- *On track for university success.* Seventy-eight percent are on track for meeting college entrance requirements for UC and CSU (they have passed thirteen or fourteen classes in the a–g sequence of courses required for admission).

Finally, an additional factor making Ag Prep stand out is its rural setting. Nearly half of all school districts in the United States are rural, and young people in those districts confront many barriers as they pursue education and careers.[15]

* * * * *

In each of the preceding examples, resourceful and thoughtful leaders have overcome barriers, whether engaging employers, aligning high school and community college curricula, convincing students and their families that investing in a technical career is a good bet for the future, or organizing existing resources into a system. Indeed, it is in organizing a system—aligning disparate components to form a coherent whole with a clear purpose—where Tennessee, Delaware, Central Ohio, Marlborough, and the Central Valley are making the most headway. Alignment may be the toughest step, the step where an outside organization like Pathways can be of help, and the step that will, if successful, ensure a sustainable system.

CHAPTER 4

WHY WORK MATTERS
IN THE LIVES OF YOUNG PEOPLE

Work-based learning has been found to increase young people's social capital, in particular courses of support and connection to postsecondary options and continuing work opportunities . . . A young person knowing that she has committed to and worked at something, coped with difficult tasks and both failed and succeeded at them, changes the way she approaches subsequent tasks, considers options, and relates to others who have committed themselves to a particular pursuit.
—Robert Halpern, *Youth, Education, and the Role of Society*

Before moving ahead to discuss the next three implementation levers in the Pathways framework—early career awareness, employer engagement, and the role of intermediary organizations—we want to first frame a core belief that underpins the Pathways Network: namely, the importance of work in human life, and especially in the development of young people. In this chapter, we explore the consequences of our persistently high youth unemployment rates, especially for those in the bottom rungs of our economy. We then review the data on the relationship between lack of economic mobility and inequality. But the primary focus of this chapter is more in the realm of the psychological than the economic: we ask what young people lose without, and what they gain developmentally and socially from, learning to work and having work experience.[1]

When we ask a typical adult audience at a Pathways event how many people had some kind of paid work experience at age sixteen or seventeen, either during the summer or after school, virtually every hand goes up. When we then show people some of the data about teen employment today, it usually comes as a shock. Only one in four sixteen- to nineteen-year-olds are getting work experience, and those from families earning $120,000 or more are more likely to have access to work than those from low-income families.[2] The message we take from the data is that if schools and employers can't join forces to provide access to some form of work experience for most young people while they are in school, those who could most benefit from it will be least likely to be able to get it on their own.

Today, millions of young Americans are stepping into the labor market after high school only to discover that the best they can do is to piece together a series of part-time, low-wage jobs that barely allow them to support themselves, much less build a satisfying life. And the same is true even among those young people with some college and no degree. These young people are at risk of diminished self-esteem and self-efficacy, not to mention a struggle for food, transportation, and housing. Indeed, career success is closely correlated with life success, and is a critical marker of achieving maturity in adulthood.[3] Young people can no longer fall back on the blue-collar jobs that once sustained those without a postsecondary credential. Those jobs have diminished in number, and low-wage service jobs have replaced them. For young people, there are negative economic consequences to swirling in the labor market for several years in their mid-twenties. Economic data shows that these lost years equal lower lifetime earnings.

If high levels of youth unemployment and the consequent loss of lifetime earnings get little attention, the issues addressed in this chapter—the harm to young people who seek employment without a broad understanding of work, workplaces, and how careers are built—get even less. These issues come under the rubric of social capital: the kinds of experiences that affluent families provide for young people through their networks, enrolling their children in enriching experiences, and supervising or guiding them through high school, college admissions, the college years, and even beyond. Low-income youth deserve the same opportunities as their more affluent peers, and, unlike in earlier decades, without a chance at good middle-skill jobs, young people face an uncertain economic future. So the challenge for educators is to better prepare working-class and poor young people not just with traditional "school knowledge," but with the experiences that will help them to understand and navigate the social worlds of mainstream institutions, those that can easily shut out the ill-prepared and ill-informed from good employment opportunities.

YOUTH EMPLOYMENT

Economist Andrew Sum (until his recent retirement, the nation's leading expert on the youth labor market) reviews the dire situation of young people seeking employment in a 2014 Brookings Foundation report, for which he was the lead author: "Employment prospects for teens and young adults in the nation's hundred largest metropolitan areas plummeted between 2000 and 2011. On a number of measures—employment rates, labor force underutilization, unemployment, and year-round joblessness—teens and young adults fared poorly, and sometimes disastrously."[4] In 2000, 44 percent of teens were in the labor market; by 2011, the figure had dropped to 24 percent. For urban, low-income teens of color, the odds of having a job—any job at all—were then at roughly 10 percent. Employment rates were lowest among teens with family incomes below $40,000, the young people most in need of earning power.[5]

And lest readers suspect that disadvantaged teens are *choosing* not to work, Sum and his colleagues provide another data point: labor market underutilization, which includes those who desire work but have stopped looking along with those who are working part-time but want full-time employment. In 2011, they note, black teens had the highest rate of underutilization (60 percent), followed by Hispanics (52 percent), Asians (48 percent), and whites (35 percent). In other words, teenagers' desire to work was as high as ever, perhaps higher. If they were not working, it was primarily because they couldn't find jobs.[6] Figure 4.1 gives more information on teen employment rates.

The aforementioned data were compiled as the country was coming out of the fiscal crisis. As the economy improved and unemployment rates fell to low levels, the heated-up labor market put in even starker relief the plight of young people. For example, in our home state, Massachusetts, the unemployment rate in March 2017 was 3.2 percent—meaning that almost everyone seeking employment has found it—but that low number has not

FIGURE 4.1   Employment, teens aged sixteen to nineteen. Employment rates of teens aged 16–19 in the nation's 100 largest metropolitan areas by educaional attainment/ school enrollment, 2000 and 2011.

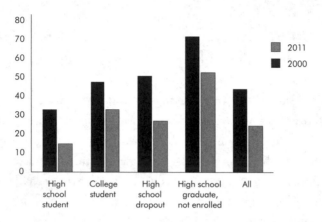

Source: Current Population Survey, Bureau of Labor Statistics. Adapted from Andrew Sum et al., *The Plummeting Labor Market Fortunes of Teens and Young Adults* (Washington, DC: Metropolitan Policy Program at Brookings Institution, 2014).

Note: Employment rates among teens declined dramatically, from 44 percent in 2000 to 24 percent in 2011, but showed variation by educational attainment and household income. Only about half of high school graduates not enrolled in postsecondary education and less than 30 percent of high school dropouts worked in a given month in 2011.

resulted in an uptick in employment for teens and young adults, particularly those of color and from low-income families.[7]

A Massachusetts research report published in fall 2016 confirms the persistence of the trend that began around 2000—fewer and fewer Massachusetts sixteen- to twenty-four-year-olds are working. Those who would benefit most—low-income young people—are the least likely to find jobs. Sixteen- to nineteen-year-olds who have experienced the steepest declines include immigrant, male, African American, and Hispanic youth. The report goes on to explain that "while some of these factors may be viewed as 'positive' things, such as the rising number of young people going to college, research does show early participation in the labor market has positive long-term impacts on young people. These positive impacts include the development of hard and soft professional skills, networking opportunities, reduced risk

FIGURE 4.2   Massachusetts employment rate (1980–2015)

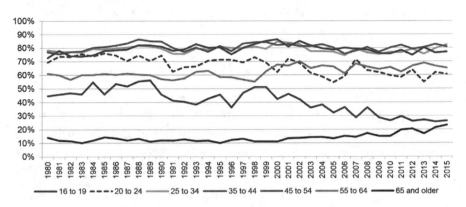

Source: Nicoya Borella, Chris Jurek, and Lindie Martin, *The Young Adult Labor Force in Massachusetts* (Hadley, MA: UMass Donahue Institute, Economic & Public Policy Research, 2016).

of negative socioeconomic outcomes and criminal behavior, and improved lifelong earning potential. These benefits are being experienced by a smaller number of young people today than in the past"[8] (see the line in figure 4.2 starting between 40 and 50 percent). We further explain these benefits in detail later in this chapter.

Youth Experience in the Labor Market

What do we know about the kinds of work experience that *are* available to sixteen- to nineteen-year-olds today? The data are clear: the percentage of young people working in low-wage jobs in the food and personal service categories (e.g., cooks, cashiers, servers, hair and beauty workers, home care aides) has risen from 15 percent in 1980 to 27 percent in 2013.[9] Thus, not only has it become much more difficult for teens to find work, but the work they do find often doesn't pay a decent wage or provide new experiences that might lead to a career choice.

According to a 2013 report from Georgetown University's Center on Education and the Workforce, *Failure to Launch: Structural Shift and the New Lost Generation*, young adults change jobs 6.3 times, on average, between the ages of eighteen and twenty-five.[10] In this environment, all young people, not just those from low-income families or with weak academic preparation, need more information about careers, more structure in their school-to-postsecondary pathways, and much more experience of the workplace than ever before. And that includes those who will become overeducated baristas or discouraged temps moving from office to office until their late twenties, despite having an associate's or a bachelor's degree.

To be clear: there is nothing inherently wrong with minimum-wage, starter jobs for teenagers, especially if a responsible adult helps them make sense of where such jobs fit in the economy and what kind of skills such jobs teach.[11] It can be motivating to find out what really makes one's juices flow as well as what is boring, unpleasant, or exploitative. But the recent decline in even low-wage service-sector opportunities means that a majority of young people from low-income backgrounds are unable to land starter jobs, which would allow them to gain initial work experience, to earn some money for living expenses and for their families, and to feel the pride that comes with a paycheck.

Their more affluent peers, especially those with social capital and family incomes in the top 5 to 10 percent, often struggle to find paying jobs, too. However, those young people are far more likely to use personal connections and adult networks to find internships, paid and volunteer, in places such as child care centers, nonprofits, scientific research labs, financial institutions, and the businesses of family and friends. For that matter, they may also get to travel abroad over the summer, participate in wilderness training, or serve as junior camp counselors, experiences that contribute to identity development and maturation—and to inequality. We explore the relationship between mobility and inequality, and how they interact with youth employment, in the next section.

MOBILITY AND INEQUALITY

When the *Pathways* report was issued in 2011, the major news outlets' headlines were far different than they are in 2017. A quick Google search for "financial crisis 2011" yields "International credit markets are showing signs of strain," "the global economy could slip back into a recession," "Dubai Financial Market downgrading US's credit rating," and "Europe 2011, a worse time than US 2008." We might say, what a difference six years makes!

Fast-forward to January 2017. *Bloomberg View* declares, "Pretty much everywhere you look—stocks, interest rates, credit derivatives—markets see a rosier picture for 2017 than they did in early November."[12] In retrospectives on his presidency, President Obama was widely praised for his leadership in pulling the United States out of the fiscal crisis. Not only has productivity gained momentum, but wages have risen slightly, unemployment is around 4.7 percent—a level not seen since 2007—and a number of states are considering laws that will raise the minimum wage. But these positive trends in the economy have had barely any impact on social mobility and inequality, and so the urgency behind the *Pathways* report is, if anything, growing greater. If the country's financial good health has had little impact on the well-being of a large percentage of the population, then what will? The answer has always been education.

The United States has long characterized itself as the country where, if you work hard in school, you can be anything you want to be. You can get rich, and you can move up the ladder from where you started. But in truth, mobility has been stagnant in the United States since the 1970s. The forces working against upward mobility are daunting, and too often not fully taken into account in the design and implementation of education programs intended to promote upward mobility. A substantial body of research documents growing inequality in the United States. By inequality, we mean the income spread between those at the bottom and those at the top. As inequality grows, the space widens between the rungs of the ladder people need to climb from their income level to the one above, impacting mobility. And because advantage grows advantage, even if there is some progress at the bottom, those in the top ranks move up at a faster rate. Today, the pace of income growth at the top is substantially higher than that at the bottom. Children born into the bottom income quintile have fallen further behind. Today only half of America's thirty-year-olds are earning more money than their parents did at the same age, declining from the 1970s, when 92 percent of thirty-year-olds earned more than their parents.[13] Thus, the United States can no longer pride itself on the idea that each generation will be more prosperous than the last.

Contrary to our view of ourselves, a recent series of international studies of economic mobility show that the United States is not the country where those born into poverty have the greatest chance of moving up in the world. As these studies have made their way into the mainstream press (see, for example, the January 4, 2012, front-page *New York Times* story, "Harder for Americans to Rise from the Lower Rungs"), Americans have had to face the fact that such "Old World" countries as Denmark, Finland, Germany, and Norway—and our New World neighbor, Canada—all have significantly higher rates of economic mobility than we do.[14] In one study, 42 percent of American men whose fathers were in the bottom fifth of the income distribution remained in the bottom fifth, while in the United Kingdom, the quintessential class-bound society we love to compare ourselves to, only 30 percent of men with fathers in the bottom quintile remained there.[15]

Here is an important and decisive factor, and one deeply influencing Pathways to Prosperity: the European countries that have higher economic mobility rates than we do also have strong vocational education systems. They start to prepare young people for the world of work early, and not just to make them widgets in the capitalist enterprise, but to equip them comprehensively for what they call "working life." These countries send a significantly smaller percentage of young people off to get purely academic degrees in a university, although in the best systems, one can move from vocational education into academic pathways. The best vocational systems are designed to align with the needs of the labor market for skilled entry-level employees with technical, communication, and workplace skills and knowledge, and they also provide general education. And they do their job. Vocational programs send young people into middle-class jobs with good wages, no matter what their family background. They help young people not only with the required skills, but also with connections to mentors—to a world beyond home and school—and they teach professional behaviors that no classroom lesson can provide. We have repeatedly asked young people apprenticing in manufacturing, carpentry, insurance, government, and health care, "Are you entering the same profession as your parents?" The answer most often was no. In fact, it's not unusual for a young person to say, as one sixteen-year-old banking apprentice did, "My father works in the forest. That is *not* what I want to do."

YOUTH DEVELOPMENT

Experiencing the workplace tends to be a prime force in helping young people grow up. Indeed, a first job is a crucial rite of passage. As Sum puts it in a 2014 report titled, disturbingly, *The Plummeting Labor Market Fortunes of Teens and Young Adults*: "Finding and keeping a job is a key step in a young person's transition to adulthood and economic self-sufficiency."[16]

Work immerses and engages young people in developmentally appropriate, real-world tasks that challenge them—not only to learn advanced subject matter, but also to regulate their behavior; complete difficult assignments; work in teams; solve the unexpected, everyday problems that occur in workplaces; and communicate effectively with colleagues of differing ages and backgrounds. Most people, especially the young, learn best through a combination of theory and practice. Practical experience—particularly job-related experience—plays a central role in the formation of personal identity. It also creates better transitions from school to the workforce.

Next we explore what young people, regardless of social class or background, learn from work experience and how to prepare them at an appropriate age to understand the choices and demands of the labor market. The literature on how high school youth develop a work identity is slim. That may be because, with the exception of some high-quality CTE programs, there is so little attention in schools to what developmental psychologist Robert Halpern calls students' "vocational selves." Yes, students often are asked about their interests, take talent inventories, or even read about careers associated with specific college majors, but that is a different matter than actually trying out skills and knowledge in a workplace. Over the years, the Pathways team has come to rely on Halpern's thinking because it provides a research-based rationale for the urgency of changing the way most young people go to high school. As Halpern notes in a 2012 article, "Schools are a central developmental institution, and it makes sense that they should play a central role in helping young people with vocationally oriented developmental tasks and try to be at least somewhat responsive to the labor market and trends in work."[17]

Yet he goes on to say, quoting Norton Grubb, that schools are "oddly removed" from the world of work; narrow disciplines are at the opposite end of the spectrum from what one encounters in a work setting, where almost all workers must draw from a varied arsenal of knowledge and experience.[18] Relatively few skills common in workplaces are integrated into curriculum. As do other researchers, Halpern notes that "decontextualized [school] learning is not effective for the majority of high school students or consistent with findings from cognitive and learning sciences that learning is most effective when it takes place in a context that allows immediate application, where young people feel some connection to real-world endeavor"—an important point signified by the use of the term "real world" as opposed to the constructed "non–real world" of school. As Halpern argues, and most adults would agree, vocations and careers have cultures, habits, practices, and ways of thinking and behaving that simply cannot be learned in an "unreal" setting.[19]

What do young people need by way of experience to support them in growing up? Most helpful, Halpern argues, are activities that take them out of their comfort zones, challenge them, place them among adult workers in authentic settings, and ask them to perform. We need to change the balance, he asserts, between in-school and out-of-school learning. School as it is currently organized has an "outsized role . . . in addressing developmental needs." Halpern makes two additional points in his argument about learning in workplaces. His first point is that workplace mentors' knowledge of their fields—their ability to model "practice, general behavior, and affective commitment" in particular fields—provides young people with a good idea of what it means to become an adult. And second, workplaces embed learning and assessment in the doing of work, with mistakes an expected part of problem solving rather than an end product that is graded but not corrected.[20]

In an influential 1991 article, "Cognitive Apprenticeship: Making Thinking Visible," John Seely Brown and colleagues argue that the traditional apprenticeship model provides the right sort of support, relying on a process of "modeling, scaffolding, fading, and coaching . . . The expert shows the apprentice how to do a task, watches as the apprentice practices portions of the task, and then turns over more and more responsibility until the apprentice is proficient enough to accomplish the task independently."[21]

Brown's goal was to translate this apprenticeship model to the school setting, but Halpern would connect it back to the workplace. Using similar language to Brown, he argues that students need many opportunities for "observing, emulating, practicing, applying, and revising," both in and out of the classroom. Schools could support the transition to working life by integrating in-school learning with out-of-school, work-based experiences that gradually lengthen as students advance toward the completion of high school and onward into postsecondary education and/or the workforce.

SOCIAL CAPITAL

In the previous section, we argue that schools can and must do a much better job of preparing young people for the world of work than they do currently. The kind of experiences Halpern and Brown promote are healthy for all young people, but they can also serve to level the playing field between those from affluent families and those who grow up in limited economic circumstances. In the final section of this chapter, we argue that the kind of work experiences described earlier in the chapter can help to mitigate social class differences by building students' social capital.

While difficult to quantify, social capital appears to be the powerful engine differentiating results on the basis of where a young person starts out. The Organization for Economic Cooperation and Development (OECD) defines social capital as "networks together with shared norms, values, and understandings that facilitate cooperation within or among groups."[22]

According to the OECD, the definition is often broken into what might be defined as concentric circles or networks composed of "bonds, bridges, and links," with the connections between each moving from family and close friends, to distant friends and colleagues, to those further up or down the social ladder.[23]

Social capital has an outsized power in helping young people develop the networks that connect them to opportunities for further learning and jobs.[24] Low-income students not only may have smaller networks initially, but may also lack the practice, experience, confidence, and resources to develop them further. They may not know how important networks and connections are. But this is clear: the greater the "dose" of social capital, the more likely a credentialed young person is to move beyond family and community bonds to activate promising connections to the labor market. Consider the powerful network of a well-resourced suburban high school attended by a majority of relatively well-off young people whose professional parents introduce their children to their colleagues and their colleagues' friends, and everyone has their eyes set on a selective four-year college. The result is a situation that sociologists label "maximally maintained inequality," described by Adam Gamoran as "a process by which privileged groups take advantage of expansion to promote the interest of their children and maintain relative advantages over less privileged groups."[25]

Professional and Social Skill Building

Current research suggests that in the next several decades, two kinds of skills will be the best predictors of workforce success: technical skills and mainstream social skills. Mainstream social skills might be labeled a subset or result of having social capital. According to numerous researchers, social skills have an increasing premium in the labor market. The change is not just from manual work to "thinking for a living," but to a labor market that increasingly rewards the skills that robots cannot easily replace because they entail understanding and managing human interaction. Economist David Deming, who has been studying the role of social skills as a valued commodity in the labor market, puts his findings this way: "Between 1980 and 2012, jobs with high social skill requirements grew by nearly 10 percentage points as a share of the US labor force. In contrast, math-intensive but less social jobs (including many STEM occupations) shrank by about 3 percentage points over the same period. Employment and wage growth was particularly strong for jobs requiring high levels of both cognitive skill and social skill."[26]

An extensive economic literature documents the return to technical and cognitive skills. Educators have interpreted this to mean that the United States needs to deepen and expand the STEM pipeline and grow new workers for labs and hospitals and other middle-skill settings. But scholars have paid less attention to the returns for social skills even though all employers say they are important. And the movement to include social and emotional learning is still in its early stages in K–12 schools.

Networks are one aspect of social capital; social skills needed to activate and participate in them are another. In 2002, sociologist Annette Lareau published a book, *Unequal Childhoods: Class, Race, and Family Life*, about family life that documented what many sense intuitively—that privilege begets privilege. It illustrates "maximally maintained inequality." Lareau is focused on how the transmission of differential advantages takes place among middle-class families. She wants to show how mainstream social skills valued in the labor force develop and are reinforced within families. In her book, she studied what she calls "the cultural logic" of parenting styles as they impact home, afterschool, and school lives of working-class and middle-class youth. She carefully documented the reasons for the higher achievement and success rates of more privileged young people.[27] Middle-class parents adopt a strategy that Lareau calls "concerted cultivation" of children. They work to "develop" children in ways that fit the standards of mainstream institutions and that benefit their children later in the work world.[28]

Lareau characterizes working-class children's parenting style as privileging "natural growth," with the result that children have long periods of unstructured time, clear boundaries exist between children and adults, and play is child-initiated without the mediating parental proviso that it be a learning experience as well. Lareau does not take an evaluative stand. She shows that these qualities have high value as children develop into independent young adults—witness the lack of independence chronicled in the lives of children with helicopter parents. Nonetheless, it is clear from her research that middle-class families do better at ensuring that their offspring meet the standards of mainstream institutions. Reconnecting in 2011 to the children she studied in 2002, Lareau shows that "the intensity of middle-class and upper-middle-class parents in building their kids' social capital only increases as children grow into young adults." As Lareau implies, middle-class parents have the resources and mindset to stay engaged in their children's lives in order to guide them and to intervene as needed long into adulthood.

Networking

We cannot count the number of times the young sons and daughters of friends or acquaintances have called us, asking politely to have dinner, to meet for some career advice, or to make a connection. These young people have firm handshakes, know how to make small talk, and are confident that they are worth our time. And of course, we are happy to be helpful. Generally, the impetus to call for advice or to make a connection comes from family. Lareau concludes that with all this parental guidance and support, "the middle-class kids generally achieved much more educational success than the working-class and low-income kids. Since education is the '800-pound gorilla' for shaping labor market chances, the career prospects of the middle-class young adults are much brighter than their less-privileged counterparts."[29]

The need for education systems to step up is clear. While educators have little capacity to create jobs, change tax policy, or slow globalization, they do have capacity to build students' social capital, to be mentors and role models, and to build confidence in their students and raise their aspirations.[30] Work experiences organized by schools and employers working together can explicitly teach young people the skills they need to navigate the broader world. In a recent study looking at data indicating that college graduates earn less if they grow up poor, the authors are trying to figure out not just if this is true, but why.[31] That's hard to do with empirical data, but their research has spawned a substantial commentary from the field, in many cases, drawn from the personal experience of those writing in.[32] What the comments add up to is that lacking mentors, connections to networks, the confidence to make calls to contacts who might help, or even the knowledge of whom to call and what to say, the storytellers simply could not overcome their class backgrounds to compete with their similarly educated peers. And without family resources to support them during a job search, they often had to take the first opportunity that came along.

As we have been told in numerous interviews with low-income young people who have had work experiences, workplaces provide advice and connections. An adult tells a summer intern: "Major in engineering—I should have. Then I wouldn't still be at this level in my job." Or, to an intern good at coding: "I'll introduce you to Ms. X, who is the best programmer in our company, and she can help you find the next job." And students respond to these new adults in their lives. Said one high school student we interviewed recently after her advanced manufacturing summer internship: "I had about four people always helping me with college choices at my company. I have all their emails and phone numbers, and we communicate."

A first-year college student, an African American man, explained: "I had two internships in high school—one in a defense attorney's office and [one in] a DA [district attorney's] office. I worked with data. I sat in on cases. I got to assist in hand-picking a jury—it was really cool. I have recommendation letters so when I'm ready to go to law school, I can use them." That student was very clear about race issues in the workplace. In answer to another question, he said, "There are not enough black lawyers in the DA's office. It's a prestigious place to work. You have to have certain grades and connections to work there. If you don't get connections, you don't get the job. You have to start from bottom and work your way up. My supervisor's last name sounded black, so she had to work as a paralegal for two years to work up. She said it would be different if she had a white last name."

We discuss employers' hesitations to work with youth throughout this book, in particular in chapter 6. Employers are correct to assume that a high school or college graduate who has only been a student will be unlikely, if hired, to quickly translate school knowledge productively to the workplace.

But it is also likely that those young people who have had the rich experiences and tutoring in mainstream social skills that more privileged families can provide still have a leg up with employers. And since these young people are the more likely ones to have internships and summer jobs, they are also likely to have "hard and soft professional skills, networking opportunities, reduced risk of negative socioeconomic outcomes and criminal behavior, and improved lifelong earning potential," as the Massachusetts report cited earlier concludes.[33] We all too often give low-income young people the message "Get a college degree, and you'll be just fine." But academic achievement alone does not guarantee success. Experience in supportive work settings scaffolded in school therefore has a disproportionately positive impact on low-income young people; it can go a long way to make up for the ways in which privilege begets privilege, and it can put young people on the road to upward mobility.

*   *   *   *   *

This chapter puts in high relief what is lost when young people arrive in their early twenties with minimal if any sustained work experience, and highlights what can be gained by early career experience. From the perspective of the welfare and healthy development of a young person, the goal of Pathways approaches is to launch all young people into their first careers. To do so, programs must ensure that young people have sufficient knowledge, skill, and social capital to enter the economy in a sector that has career ladders, and are prepared to choose a next step.

CHAPTER 5

ENSURING CAREER AWARENESS, EXPOSURE, AND WORK-BASED LEARNING

Work-based learning provides an array of both broad and very particular "meta-lessons" about work, workplaces, and vocations. Young people learn that tasks and problems in work settings are rarely as neatly defined as those in the classroom . . . Young people learn that almost any field is deeper than it seems from the outside, and a field that may have seemed mundane has many elements that make it interesting to consider.

—Robert Halpern, *Youth, Education, and the Role of Society*

Work-based learning, a sequenced and coordinated set of activities through which students gain increasing exposure to the world of work, addresses a shared goal of educators and employers: preparing students with the knowledge, skills, and behaviors needed for productive careers. As we have discussed, opportunities to engage in meaningful work experiences help students develop both technical skills and twenty-first-century skills, including the maturity needed to work collaboratively, solve problems, and follow assignments through to completion.

Work-based learning sits at the intersection of two of the five levers of the Pathways framework, career readiness and employer engagement. In this chapter, we describe the ideal work-based learning continuum of career awareness, exploration, preparation, and training experiences and look in-depth at the state of work-based learning in the United States. Next, we explore impact, barriers to implementation, and strong case examples of work-based learning across the continuum, including one model, the Wonderful Company's Ag Prep Academy, that moves students along the entire continuum.

THE WORK-BASED LEARNING CONTINUUM

The most effective work-based learning takes the form of a continuum of activities, set out as a sequence generally accepted in the field as good practice:

1. Students begin with *career awareness and exploration* through activities such as engaging with guest speakers and going on field trips.
2. They then transition to *career preparation* activities, such as working with industry mentors and completing internships.
3. Finally, the *career training* phase of the continuum prepares students for work in specific occupations.

Students should be engaged in this continuum beginning no later than in the middle grades and should continue with work-based learning through high school and into postsecondary education. Employer engagement at all points along this continuum is essential in order to ensure that students receive up-to-date information, acquire skills aligned with industry needs, and have opportunities to learn about the world of work from professionals in the field. While there are still variants on the continuum of activities, figure 5.1 is among the most commonly used. Note that phases of the continuum overlap, and extend through at least the first two years of postsecondary education.[1] As with most such schema, while it is useful as a formulation of the ideal, application among those creating career-focused grade 9–14 pathways is a much more complicated and demanding matter.

REALITIES OF WORK-BASED LEARNING

In our work over the last five years to develop grade 9–14 pathways, both challenges and gaps have appeared in the implementation of work-based learning. Challenges range from, on the school side, the overemphasis on academic subjects to, on the employer side, hesitancy to allow teenagers into places of business. Ironically, it is kindergarteners and first graders who take field trips to the fire station, the airport, the bakery, or the hospital to learn about such places, and middle schoolers who are judged too old

FIGURE 5.1 The work-based learning continuum

Career Awareness	Career Exploration	Career Preparation: Practicum and Internships	Career Training
Learning ABOUT work Build awareness of the variety of careers available and the role of postsecondary education; broaden student options.	**Learning ABOUT work** Explore career options and postsecondary for the purpose of motivating students and to inform their decision making in high school and postsecondary education.	**Learning THROUGH work** Apply learning through practical experience that develops knowledge and skills necessary for success in careers and postsecondary education.	**Learning FOR work** Train for employment and/or postsecondary education in a specific range of occupations.
Sample student learning outcome Student can articulate the type of postsecondary education and training required in the career field and its importance to success in that field.	*Sample student learning outcome* Student can give at least two examples of how the student's individual skills and interests relate to the career field and/or occupations.	*Sample student learning outcome* Student builds effective collaborative working relationships with colleagues and customers; is able to work with diverse teams, contributing appropriately to the team effort.	*Sample student learning outcome* Student demonstrates knowledge and skills specific to employment in a range of occupations in a career field.
Experience defined by: •One-time interaction with partner(s), often for a group of students • Designed primarily by adults to broaden student's awareness of a wide variety of careers and occupations	*Experience defined by:* •One-time interaction with partner(s) for a single student or small group • Personalized to connect to emerging student interests. • Student takes an active role in selecting and shaping the experience • Depth in particular career fields. • Builds skills necessary for in-depth work-based learning	*An experience differentiated by:* • Direct interaction with partners over time • Application of skills transferable to a variety of careers • Activities have consequences and value beyond success in the classroom. • Learning for student and benefit to partner are equally valued	*An experience differentiated by:* • Interaction with partners over extended period of time • Benefit to the partner is primary and learning for student is secondary • Develop mastery of occupation specific skills • Complete certifications or other requirements of a specific range of occupations
Experiences might include: • Workplace tour • Guest speaker • Career fair • Visit parents at work	*Experiences might include:* • Informational interview • Job shadow • Virtual exchange with a partner	*Experiences might include:* • Integrated project with multiple interactions with professionals • Student-run enterprise with partner involvement • Virtual enterprise or other extended online interactions with partners • Projects with partners through industry student organizations • Service learning and social enterprises with partners •Compensated internship connected to curriculum	*Experiences might include:* • Internship required for credential or entry to occupation • Apprenticeship • Clinical experience • On-the-job training

Source: College & Career Academy Support Network, University of California, Berkeley, http://casn.berkeley.edu/resource_files/work_based_learning_continuum.pdf.

for these experiences. While trips to science museums, aquariums, and historic sites are certainly educational, they are rarely visited for purposes other than learning new academic content, although they, too, are staffed by people who have chosen engaging careers and could talk with students about their work. By high school, if there are field trips, they are usually either social events or focused on bringing academic content to life in museums or through travel—a worthy goal, but not one that contributes to explicit career exploration.

One critical goal of Pathways to Prosperity—some might argue the most critical—is to engage almost all students in work experience, embedding the continuum of activities in figure 5.1 during the years between sixth or seventh grades and an associate's degree. From four years of asset mapping where we always investigate early career advising and awareness activities, we identified an almost universal gap in middle school attention to careers. (We describe a Pathways middle school curriculum, "Possible Futures, Possible Selves," our emerging solution to that problem, later in this chapter.) While it is difficult to generalize about the high schools and districts we have visited, it would be fair to say that, with the exception of strong vocational schools and high schools designed specifically to introduce students to a sector or industry, none offer widespread career exploration or preparation, and very few offer or link students with paid internships.

CAREER AWARENESS AND EXPLORATION: GETTING TO KNOW THE WORLD OF WORK

The earlier parts of the continuum—career awareness and exploration—are less of a challenge for schools to set up and support than those later in the continuum, such as full-scale practicums, internships, or apprenticeships. (As we explain in chapter 6, the latter have high yield for young people, but require more structure and commitment on the part of employers and education institutions.) Among the most frequently implemented awareness and exploration strategies are enabling students to participate in career fairs, having speakers visit classrooms, or, more complex but of greater impact, organizing short-term company visits and more individualized job shadows.

Well scaffolded in the school curriculum and followed by a structured time for reflection on preassigned research and observation goals, these kinds of activities can introduce young people to the cultures, behaviors, and textures of work in various industry sectors. Although rarely the case today, job shadows and speaker visits can be used as an explicit strategy to help young people build social networks, a form of social capital. Most importantly, they can help students heighten their aspirations. It's one thing to observe in an advanced manufacturing plant or bank, and another to introduce yourself to a host with a handshake, explain your interest in the company, and ask for a card or inquire about summer jobs. And it's yet one more step to understand why such behaviors are important, and finally to imagine yourself in the host's place as an adult.

There are good examples of high school career awareness and exploration activities in such career-focused high schools as NAF academies, Linked Learning schools in California, the High Schools That Work network, P-TECH schools, Big Picture schools, and many specialized CTE schools.[2] One can also see high-quality integration of career exploration with academics in schools like High Tech High, the subject of the film *Most Likely to Succeed*. Such activities also exist in STEM-themed schools including health and engineering schools or academies.

Barriers to Career Awareness and Exploration

While simpler than those that involve more employer engagement, awareness and exploration activities are challenging to implement for a variety of reasons. Career exploration activities are often the purview of school guidance departments, but in general, the guidance staff is stretched thin and focused on college applications, academic and behavior problems, and mental health emergencies. In addition, few guidance counselors have firsthand knowledge of the requirements of middle-skill jobs or the pathways to them. Thus, without a system for linking schools and employers, teachers are left to reach out randomly to find speakers, often a frustrating and time-consuming task that takes more energy than it is worth if not part of a well-thought-out curriculum.

As core requirements fill up the majority of the school day, and curriculum within each discipline has "coverage" requirements, teachers may feel that career exploration simply will take away from the learning outcomes for which they are accountable. Additionally, asking teachers to connect directly with employers and build curriculum around work is like asking a math teacher to teach English. Most teachers have been in their career for the better part of their working lives, and are not conversant enough with the world of work to be able to build in appropriate activities or projects, let alone find the best speakers or sites for visits.

Some states and regions are setting up "matching" platforms where businesses willing to participate in school visits and projects can register so that teachers can contact them. These may provide some help, but it is too soon to know. There are also a growing number of small for-profit and nonprofit organizations, generally place based, offering services to match students with opportunities in specific sectors—most notably IT. The following are two best-practice examples of career awareness and exploration programs, which happen to fall at each end of the pathways grades spectrum, middle school and postsecondary.

Program Showcase: Career Awareness and Exploration

Possible Futures, Possible Selves: Filling the middle school gap in career awareness[3]

The Pathways team anticipated fairly well what would be needed to create career pathways, but one large gap that we hadn't considered appeared during asset mapping across member states and regions: career advising and awareness were critically understaffed and underresourced in the middle grades. Thus, even in districts where high schools did carry out awareness and exploration activities in ninth and tenth grades, most students were unprepared to make a good choice.

Responding to this demand, the Pathways to Prosperity Network, with support from the Noyce Foundation, initiated the development of "Possible

Futures, Possible Selves," a middle school career awareness and exploration curriculum. Through projects, simulations, and career and college visits, middle schoolers become "young professionals." As they complete challenges based on relevant, real-world problems, they build the foundation for critical thinking, collaboration, and innovation. While this is not workplace learning, it sets the stage in an age-appropriate way for students to begin to understand and experience the world of work.

Possible Futures career modules focus on three STEM fields: health sciences, IT, and engineering. Students hone their twenty-first-century skills as they apply design thinking or the engineering design cycle to dream up and create solutions to problems contextualized in the world of careers. Whether becoming young coders and designing apps to solve a community need or supporting a patient's recovery as allied health workers, young participants experience STEM activities tuned to the STEM careers that shape our world. For some youth, exploring the world of STEM careers holds special complexity; they do not see themselves in the STEM fields. Through Possible Futures, students not only see diverse images of STEM professionals, but also explore how they could make powerful contributions to their communities.

At the time of this writing, Possible Futures is being piloted in twenty-seven middle schools across three districts. During each cycle of feedback, Possible Futures has incorporated changes based on educators' experiences implementing the curricula. The field highlighted a need for resources for multiple learning environments, including extended learning time. Through a partnership with Citizen Schools, Possible Futures adapted career exploration modules for extended day learning and piloted them in extended/afterschool and summer programs. In addition, Possible Futures has added a Skills for Success module to develop those competencies that we prefer to call "professional" rather than "soft" skills and researchers refer to as "non-cognitive" skills.

Schools across the Pathways Network also highlighted the uneven abilities of counselors and families to expose students to modern career options. The Lenses on the Future module offers three lenses for youth to view their current options and navigate future opportunities: self, society, and security. These lenses support families and educators as they offer informal guidance to students. Possible Futures is piloting school-to-home connections—inviting contributions from families as young people explore their current values and future options. Possible Futures encourages schools to reevaluate the notion that education occurs before—and separate from—careers. When aligned to opportunities in STEM fields and the labor market, this approach shows potential to improve outcomes both for youth and for their communities, which need their promise and talent.

Guttman Community College's answer to the career challenge: Helping college students learn about work[4]

While the goal of the pathways movement is for all students to gain meaningful work experience on the way to a two-year degree, attaining such a goal is a long way off. Accordingly, we need to develop alternatives or complements to work experience. Building on the themes in chapter 4 of how exposure to work affects young adults, we profile Guttman Community College, the first new college in the City University of New York (CUNY) system in forty years. Guttman was designed to introduce students to the integral connection between intellectual exploration, acquisition of concrete skills and knowledge, and career development. Now in its third year, the college has a philosophical and pedagogical commitment to experiential and workplace learning combined with rigorous academics. All Guttman students attend full time their first year, and all have enrolled with the understanding that the college will prepare them for a limited number of career areas—all areas of job growth for New York City—as well as for transfer to four-year institutions.[5] At the time of this writing, the student body is under one thousand, but the college will grow to around five thousand. Students come from all boroughs of New York, generally immediately from high school; 85 percent are nineteen or younger. The student body is about 55 percent Hispanic, 26 percent African American, and 13 percent white, with a small number of Pacific Islanders, and there is substantial language diversity. The majority of students are female.

The college has had only four graduating classes. The good news is that two-year graduation rates are higher than anticipated (35 percent in 2015), and substantially higher than CUNY community colleges in the aggregate. While still early in the college's history, there is much to learn from its approach to launching young people into careers. One might state the hypothesis behind Guttman's curriculum as: *Students who understand the meaning of work in human lives, the sociology of the professions, and who have some professional work experience will have greater agency in entering the labor market than those who believe only a credential is needed. In addition, students who understand the challenges that being a member of a marginalized group impose in the work world—being working class or dark skinned or speaking with an accent—will, armed with that knowledge, enter the job market more successfully.*

Students take three courses in the first year: Statistics, City Seminar (about New York City topics such as sustainability, food, housing, gentrification, consumerism, and immigration), and Ethnographies of Work (EOW). EOW gives students tools for understanding and addressing the challenges and opportunities they face in the labor market, but it does so in both a theoretical and applied context—students interview people doing jobs of interest to them, but they also read ethnographic studies, books like *Gig: Americans Talk About Their Jobs*, and Marx and Weber.[6] The first-semester EOW course description is as follows:

Ethnographies of Work I introduces students to sociological and anthropological perspectives on work as they investigate a range of careers. The course approaches work as a cultural system invested with meanings, norms, values, customs, behavioral expectations, and social hierarchies. Students pose key questions through the lens of ethnography in order to investigate workplaces, occupations, and career pathways in an urban context. Guided by the ethnographer's assumption that there's "always more than meets the eye," students are encouraged to uncover myths and stereotypes about the work world and gain appreciation of how and why work matters to individuals in a range of occupations. Students explore dimensions of work life in the context of contemporary dynamics of disruption, uncertainty, innovation, and diversity, and draw connections between the self and work through readings, films, interviews, and fieldwork. The centerpiece of the course is for students to compose and present ethnographic accounts of workplace relations and vocational pathways as they contemplate their own career journeys.

The course is generating considerable interest nationally for several reasons. First, it addresses the teaching of professional skills by taking them out of isolated workshops and embedding them in a larger sociological understanding of how these skills work in society, how they are valued, what class and race narratives accompany them, and how the labor market responds to their absence or presence. EOW is so interesting because it makes learning about work both an intellectual and experiential endeavor at the center of the curriculum. Teaching ethnographic methods heightens students' capacity to observe, to treat a workplace as a theatre where meanings are nuanced and must be found out. The course also raises a provocative question: Can engaging the subject of work as a key aspect of human lives develop students' confidence and competence about entering the labor market? Can it attune students to mitigate problems they may encounter as a result of being working class, female, or dark skinned, or of speaking with an accent when job hunting? Build their confidence in using networks? Help students internalize and effortlessly use the requisite "professional skills" employers seek? Will they be able to better advocate for themselves armed with analytical tools learned and practiced in college?

EOW is also being taught in a New York City early college high school, with positive results, and replications are under way elsewhere in New York and out of state. The message we take from this example is that creativity is needed to help all young people learn about work, and at best, experience and reflect on it during their teenage years. Even if employers sign on to create a pipeline of young professionals in whose learning they invest, it will take years for opportunities to reach significant scale. The pathways movement needs to encourage courses like ethnographies of work, startups creating virtual work experiences, and the expansion of student-run businesses like the credit unions, restaurants, helpdesk, and web design services run by, from, and within high schools. And Pathways proponents need to persist in making the case that everyone wins when young people learn about and experience the satisfaction of having a good internship and first job experience.

CAREER PREPARATION AND TRAINING: THE IMPACT OF INTERNSHIPS

Further along the continuum of work-based learning are experiential learning experiences, such as internships, which provide participants with an opportunity to learn about a career or industry by working for an employer for a limited period of time. Internships enable participants to gain applied experience, build professional and technical skills, and make connections in a field of interest. An internship may spark a high school student's interest in a field, encouraging him to complete high school and enroll in postsecondary education.[7] However, there is little literature about the impact on career choices and aspirations of young people who have experienced high school internships, especially as concerns the contexts for noncognitive skills development.[8] Yet these experiences remain critical—a survey by the National Association of Colleges and Employers found that more than 65 percent of students with paid internships received full-time job offers, as compared with 39 percent of students with no internship experience.[9]

Barriers to Career Preparation and Training

Many employers are hesitant to engage at the more intense end of the continuum, and especially to offer internships, due to perceived barriers such as safety regulations and liability issues. Yet, if students are to have access to the full continuum of work-based learning activities, it is essential to address employers' concerns and possible—or perceived—barriers.[10]

The trouble with internships

Clearly, the most challenging goal in the career preparation continuum is the internship. Few organizations working on pathways have defined "internship" in such a way that employers know what they are being asked to provide. While the "gold standard" is a full-time paid internship lasting a number of weeks, preferably in the summer between junior and senior years, few employers are prepared to provide anything like that even on a limited scale. NAF has gone furthest, we believe, in defining an ample internship in a useful way, but again is far from making such an experience universally available in their nearly six hundred NAF academies. The criteria include:

- compensation of no less than the federal (or local, if higher) subminimum training wage;
- duration of 120 hours, which may consist of two assessed 60+ hour internships;
- direct supervision by an accountable adult who is not the student's teacher;
- the production of work that is valuable to the employer; and
- a written individualized learning plan targeted to work-based learning outcomes.[11]

Where work experiences are available at scale, typically in the summer, public-private partnerships generally are the best managers. The organization in the Pathways Network with the most successful long-term experience in such partnerships is the Boston Private Industry Council (PIC), profiled in chapter 6. The PIC's infrastructure is supported by state dollars that enable PIC staff to work with employers to place students; employers pay the wages.

Along with the challenge of signing up employers, especially large ones, to take on more than two or three students comes the even more difficult task of linking the job to the student's area of interest. In some instances, educators and employers exploit the potential for career-focused learning and reflection through workshops and explicit mentoring, but broad-scale internship programs are often no more and no less than summer job placements.

Competition between low-income and affluent teens for internships and jobs

In addition to the challenges of access, funding, and integrating learning goals, summer jobs programs for low-income young people compete with the many opportunities available to young people from families of means.

Cities like Boston (twelve thousand summer jobs for youth), New York (sixty thousand), Chicago (twenty-five thousand), and Los Angeles (eleven thousand) are seeking places for low-income high school students, perhaps lacking some social skills and having perceived academic deficits, against a market that often prefers a prep schooler or someone who has already "aced" multiple AP courses.[12] The Internet is filled with expensive high school internship placement enterprises that specialize, as do the private services that prep the affluent for college admission, in setting up privileged young people with a summer job or internship. These programs provide great fodder for college admission essays as well as preparation to go to the front of the queue for jobs later on. Not only are these summer programs for the privileged, but so are the options they offer, which certainly do not appear on the roster of a summer jobs program for low-income youth.

Despite these barriers, career preparation and training opportunities like internships are flourishing in some Pathways schools and beyond. Next we profile two interesting programs.

Program Showcase: Career Preparation and Training

Work experience for low-income youth: Cristo Rey school

One small recent study of eighteen high schoolers at a Cristo Rey school points to the importance of work experience for low-income youth. Within the network of Cristo Rey schools, working one day a week, four students share a corporate job that would otherwise be done by an entry-level employee. The company pays the usual salary, which goes toward tuition at the Catholic school. All students work all four years of high school and participate once a week in a seminar to reflect on their work experience. The school uses the experience primarily to support students in developing the noncognitive skills so important to their futures. While the study sought to understand the impact of the school as a whole, fourteen of the eighteen students mentioned the work-based learning experience as particularly important preparation for post–high school life. Said one young woman looking back at the work experience: "Being out there in the corporate world, being able to have, like corporate communications, knowing how to be professional and knowing how to tone down your attitude . . . Once you step in the door, like I said . . . it's not about you anymore. It's about who's the client for the day."

Said another: "Like socially, it helped me talk to adults, because I was so used to talking with people my age, and my boss was like fifty, and I had no idea how really to approach her . . . but after the two years, we became really close, and she was almost like a second mother to me, because she gave me a lot of advice."

The team studying Cristo Rey, a group of experts in positive youth development, lists a broad set of skills looking across their interviews and the developing literature on the topic:

> Our alumni fit the descriptions of "gritty" youth, who demonstrate the capacity to regulate their time, attention, emotions, and social interactions, and sustain perseverance, despite ongoing life challenges. In addition to the intrapersonal skills associated with self-control and self-awareness, many of these young people described confidence in their social and interpersonal competencies, as well as capacities for self-reflection and self- and other awareness, which have been identified as important competencies in research on social and emotional learning and for career decision making. In this sense, these young people appear to be equipped with a number of the twenty-first-century skills which many employers observe as lacking in young people today.[13]

Graduating with a path forward: Delaware's manufacturing internship[14]

A growing summer program in Delaware exemplifies the optimal connection between a high school curriculum and a summer internship. Five years ago, high school students had no option to train for manufacturing careers in Delaware. By the summer of 2015, the state's community college, Delaware Technical Community College (Del Tech), had worked with local companies such as Siemens, Bloom Energy, Agilent Technologies, and AstraXeneca to place their first cohort of rising high school seniors in paid summer internships with local manufacturing companies. These students are on their way to completing Del Tech's Advanced Manufacturing Pathways Program. Within the next three years, an additional 150 students will complete internships and graduate ready for jobs or additional education in this high-demand field. In the 2016–17 school year, nearly six thousand students in twenty-nine of forty-four high schools are enrolled in state-model pathways programs.

Delaware chose manufacturing as a starting place. Over the past decade, facing the demise of manufacturing, General Motors, Chrysler, and other heavy industry manufacturers left the state. But recently, small- and medium-size tech-enabled specialty manufacturers have joined the Delaware economy, creating a skills gap within this reemerging industry. Del Tech designed the Advanced Manufacturing Pathways Program to address this identified skills gap and respond to the need for a pipeline of manufacturing workers who possess an increased level of technical skills. With funding from a Trade Adjustment Assistance Community College and Career Training (TAACCCT) grant, the college launched a manufacturing technician program for adult learners in 2011. The curriculum, equipment, and lab for this program became the foundation for its Advanced Manufacturing Pathways Program for high school students.

Del Tech implemented a unique dual enrollment program that allows for high school juniors and seniors to split time between their high school and Del Tech's Innovation Technology Center. Students receive over six hundred hours of instruction utilizing curricula crafted by both industry experts and the College's Center for Creative Instruction and Technology. Integrating traditional classroom teaching methods with a state-of-the-art Amatrol simulated training platform helps to produce learning experiences that mirror the technology in the workplace. To further complement this work-based learning experience, students complete a two-hundred-hour paid craftsmanship experience at the end of their first year of instruction. By the completion of the two-year program, students earn national certifications and are eligible for advanced standing with up to thirteen college credits toward programs at Del Tech, providing a path to both postsecondary education and immediate employment in the manufacturing field.

Del Tech mounted the first substantial manufacturing pathway very quickly—employers were waiting eagerly for graduates. This past June, out of the first cohort of twenty-four graduates, eight were immediately hired to work in manufacturing, sixteen are attending Del Tech, and six are enrolled in a four-year institution. Several of those at the four-year college are also working, and they are great ambassadors for the program that has sent them on productive career pathways that most had never anticipated.

THE CONTINUUM OF WORK-BASED LEARNING IN PRACTICE

The Pathways Network is only five years old, and the goal of building a system of grade 9–14 career-focused pathways will take at least a decade to fully realize. Nonetheless, in some Network sites we can already begin to see what a fully operational system of pathways might look like. Here, we briefly describe how the Wonderful Company is structuring a continuum of work-based learning activities into its Agriculture Prep academies.[15] A design like this could serve as a model across the Network.

Program Showcase: Wonderful Ag Prep

Wonderful Ag Prep Academy guarantees paid internships to all twelfth graders who fulfill the program requirements, but this culminating experience and privilege is scaffolded by carefully planned work experiences leading up to the internship. The following is an edited version of the Wonderful Company's brief on job shadowing written by a JFF consultant.[16]

Ag Prep's work-based learning sequence in the agriculture industry

For each year of high school, Ag Prep provides students with a unique off-campus learning experience in the agriculture industry. These hands-on, work-based learning opportunities are integrated into Ag Prep's overall college and career strategy and are tailored to the student's pathway of study. There are four phases of Ag Prep's work-based learning sequence in the ag industry:

- *Freshman year: Ag conferences.* All ninth graders attend a prominent ag industry conference in California (such as the World Ag Expo, the

Almond Board Food Quality and Safety Symposium, and the AgSafe Convention), where they meet with ag professionals and learn about career opportunities.

- *Sophomore year: Job shadows.* All sophomores participate in two intensive job shadowing experiences with mid-level managers at an ag company.
- *Junior year: Mentorships.* All juniors participate in a sustained mentorship with a senior manager, including interview practice, career guidance, and feedback on capstone projects.
- *Senior year: Paid internships.* All seniors who fulfill the program's requirements are guaranteed a paid internship with the Wonderful Company.

Developing the Ag Prep job shadowing program

Ag Prep developed its job shadowing program over a number of years. Supervisors at the Wonderful Company have worked with high school teachers and college faculty on Pathway Advisory Committees since 2014–15. Through a guided process, the Pathway Advisory Committees members created skills maps for each of Ag Prep's three pathways (plant science, agriculture mechanics, and business management, leading to jobs such as irrigation manager, equipment mechanic, and accountant or analyst) to help align the curriculum with the skills needed for well-paying careers and with the rigors of university expectations.[17] The skills maps helped identify gaps in the traditional high school curriculum that the work-based learning sequence could help to address.

Drawing from the committees' work, Ag Prep developed a job shadowing program that included a process for engaging with its company and school partners to:

- build their commitments to the program;
- prepare host employees and students for the experience; and
- follow up with the hosts and students afterward.

The program was piloted in 2015–16 and was expanded in 2016–17 to a two-day experience for all sophomores.

Ag Prep staff members meet at least annually with executive leadership at the Wonderful Company and Olam International, another Central Valley agriculture company, to confirm their commitment to the shadowing experience, and more frequently with supervisors (in most cases, the human resources director) to set specific goals and address logistics. The skills maps have been crucial in laying the groundwork for a common language during these discussions. Choosing specific skills to address during the job shadowing experience helps the company supervisors decide which employees to select for job shadowing—that is, those who best exhibit the skills identified and who are most appropriate for interacting with high school students.

Preparing employees for job shadowing day

Host employees are selected at mid-level positions, such as managers, directors, analysts, and crew leaders. Ag Prep meets with host employees about a week prior to the event to review the job shadowing goals and design, answer questions, and gather information about each employee. Employees discuss the specific skills they will be addressing.

Prepping students for job shadowing day

Ag Prep also meets with students to explain the upcoming experience, conduct safety training, answer questions, share links to reading material about the company, and provide information about the host employees. The students participate in role playing to prepare them for success in a work environment: practicing a firm handshake, using direct eye contact, and asking appropriate questions.

In both the company and school settings, Ag Prep has found it crucial to explain that job shadowing is neither a PowerPoint presentation nor a field trip. In particular:

- *Ag Prep encourages employees not to vary their day significantly.* Employees tend to think of their own days as routine, and they may want to spice things up for students. However, the activities they do *routinely* are precisely the ones that students need and want to see.

- *Ag Prep works with students in advance to prepare questions for industry hosts.* Many students are intimidated by the prospect of conversing with a professional for several hours. However, asking questions and engaging in conversation one-on-one is precisely the experience that is transformative for students.

The job shadowing experience

Ag Prep's students shadow a mid-level employee throughout the workday, in an occupation aligned with their pathway of study. Each host employee is paired with only two students, so that each student can engage extensively with the employee while witnessing the activities and tasks associated with the job. The hosts are encouraged to perform their regular duties and converse with students about their job and career. The day is highly structured, yet the shadowing experience is personalized, based on the hosts' job routines. Students and employees share box lunches for an informal moment together.

Ag Prep follows up with students and employees after each event, and improves the experience based on their feedback. During the debrief activity at the end of the day, the students reflect on their experience. Afterward, they write a thank-you card to their host employee and they submit a five-hundred- to one-thousand-word personal narrative online about the impact of the experience on their future plans. Said one, "After going to a lab, I realized that I can use math in my everyday job—and English, because if you're behind a desk all day you communicate with people and you write." Said a second, "I thought that agriculture was picking grapes and working machines. But then she [turned on] her computer and all these numbers came up . . . I never knew there was that part to agriculture." Each employee provides written comments on the participation and skills exhibited by their students.

*   *   *   *   *

Possible Futures, Possible Selves, Delaware manufacturing pathways, and Ag Prep are ahead of the curve in conceptualizing and carrying out a set of high-impact career exploration and work-based learning experiences that change the way young people go to school. But the work in these places has lessons for all. The great resource of the Pathways to Prosperity Network is that among the participants, we can count on a person or a group to refine and document practices that are useful to all. And indeed, Ag Prep held an invitational conference in Los Angeles in 2016 to acquaint leaders with their work; Delaware hosted the entire Pathways to Prosperity Network for site visits and discussion in spring 2017; and Possible Future, Possible Selves is moving from pilot to broad implementation. With robust work-based learning practices like these made available to all, the Pathways to Prosperity Network can help push this important lever in expanding meaningful exposure to work experiences to more and more youth.

CHAPTER 6

THE ROLE OF EMPLOYERS AND INTERMEDIARY ORGANIZATIONS IN PATHWAYS SYSTEMS

Over the last several years, we had the good fortune to participate in two international studies of career and technical education that have provided us the opportunity to visit strong systems in several European and Asian countries.[1] Between us we have studied vocational education and training (VET) in Australia, China, Finland, Germany, the Netherlands, Norway, Singapore, Sweden, and Switzerland. In some of these systems, VET is primarily school based; in others, it is primarily work based, with students spending three days a week in a firm and the other two days in vocational schools. In virtually all of these systems, however, employers take a more active role than in the United States in shaping programs to ensure that they are well aligned with entry requirements for employment in their occupational sector and in providing well-structured short-term internships or more extended apprenticeships. Consequently, the graduates of these programs, which typically serve between 30 and 70 percent of the upper secondary age cohort (equivalent to grades 10–12 in the United States), make a much smoother transition into the labor market by their early twenties than do similar young Americans.

It is difficult to compare our American high school CTE programs with VET programs in these other systems. In the United States, as previously noted, a CTE concentrator is someone who takes three or more courses in a particular occupational area. This means students can be counted as concentrators if CTE courses make up only one-fifth of their high school schedules. Contrast this with Switzerland, for example, where over three or four years, at least 60 percent of a VET student's time is spent in eight-hour days at the worksite, supplemented by additional classroom hours in which some of the time is devoted to vocational topics. Hence, in the draft interim report of its 2010 *Learning for Jobs* study, the Organization for Economic Cooperation and Development (OECD) concluded that fewer than 1 percent of US high school students were in vocational education. US government officials reacted in disbelief to what they thought was a huge error, pointing out that in fact something like one-quarter of American students were CTE concentrators. OECD staff responded that in international terms the CTE "dosage" that US students receive is so minimal that it barely registers. (The final report resolved the issue by omitting the United States from the bar graph comparing the percentage of students in vocational education in each participating country.)

Why is the United States such an outlier in international comparisons of vocational education? In our view the explanation has a lot to do with the major transition that has taken place in the US economy over the last fifty years. In 1973, only one-third of jobs required any education beyond high school, so most students with some vocational education could leave high school and move directly into a good job in a factory or an office that could put them on a path to a middle-class living. In today's economy, by contrast, only one-third of jobs are available to those with only a high school diploma, and those are mostly low-skill, minimum-wage jobs that do not start a young person on a path to a family-supporting income.

As we noted in chapter 1, the growing focus in the 1980s and 90s on raising academic standards and improving performance in the core academic subjects drove out space for electives in most comprehensive high schools, causing a sharp decline in vocational course taking and opportunities for workplace learning. As the pendulum has swung back in the last few years and career academies and other career-focused programs have come more into vogue, they have been introduced primarily as a strategy for engaging students and motivating them to complete high school rather than as a strategy for preparing them for employment. Even full-time vocational schools no longer see themselves as primarily in business to prepare young people to enter the workforce straight out of high school. The best such schools now pride themselves on having high postsecondary enrollment rates, understanding that their graduates, even those with industry certifications, will be best served in the labor market with some kind of postsecondary credential as well.

The differences in the intensity, duration, structure, and purpose of vocational programs in the United States and some of the strongest European and Asian nations are reflected in the very different roles employers play in these systems. In American CTE programs, the primary role for employers is to serve on advisory committees. Any program that receives federal funds through the Perkins Act is required to have an industry advisory committee. In strong vocational high schools, these committees can be very active, meeting regularly to ensure that the programs they advise stay current with the changing job requirements in their industry. At their best, these committees also help provide internships and other work experience opportunities, equipment donations, teacher externships in industry, and other program enhancements. More typically, however, industry advisory committees take a far less active role. Because they are advisory only, their members show up for meetings when asked but feel little sense of ownership or responsibility for program direction. Because vocational programs in the United States sit fully inside the education system, it is up to the educators to reach out if they want to engage employers as genuine partners in program design and management.

In this chapter, we explore the role of employers in international VET systems, then contrast it to how US employers have traditionally interacted with CTE and education and training systems. However, as we show in several employer exemplar profiles, progress is being made in employer engagement, as well as through employer industry associations, which help bring this work to scale. Finally, we explain the role of intermediary organizations, which often play the role of translator or liaison between education and industry.

EMPLOYER ROLES IN STRONG VOCATIONAL EDUCATION AND TRAINING SYSTEMS[2]

In the international "dual system" countries, where students spend at least half their time in learning at a workplace and the rest in school, employers and their industry associations play a very different role. They are full partners with educators and government officials in the design and management of vocational educational programs. They take the lead in setting program standards and defining the skills and competencies young people must be able to demonstrate for successful entry into their industry. They participate in the assessment process, serving with educators on panels to examine student work in order to certify that it meets industry standards. And most important, employers not only provide paid apprenticeships for young people, but also train coaches and supervisors to ensure that the apprenticeship experience is designed to support the young person's learning and development goals while contributing to the firm's bottom line.

Employers and their associations take this kind of active leadership role in VET systems in countries like Austria, Germany, the Netherlands, and Switzerland for a mix of reasons. For some firms, especially smaller ones, apprenticeship programs make good financial sense. Given the substantial difference between apprentice wages and the starting wages of full-time workers, cost-benefit analyses have demonstrated that by the end of a typical three-year program, the training costs to the company, including apprentice wages, have been more than offset by the gains in productivity. This is because, by the middle of the second year, the typical apprentice is as productive as a regular starting employee. This means that even if the firm has no full-time opening to offer the young person at the end of the apprenticeship, the investment has still more than paid for itself.

For most firms offering apprenticeships, however, a primary motive is recruitment. What better way to build a pipeline of talented, dedicated future employees than to train them yourself and have three or four years to assess their performance and potential for growth before committing to hiring them? This motive is especially powerful in a country like Germany, which has a highly regulated labor market. In such markets, it is difficult and expensive to fire an employee, so getting to know a young person very well before hiring them greatly reduces the risk of making a very expensive mistake. In Switzerland, whose labor market is much less regulated, this motive is less important, and thus there is less pressure for companies to hold onto their own apprentices after graduation. It is not uncommon to hear Swiss employers say that they will sometimes encourage even their strong apprentices to seek experience elsewhere, believing that they will ultimately be more valuable employees if and when they return.

In strong VET systems, employers approach participation in vocational education and training as an opportunity to shape their future workforce. They believe that socializing young people into the world of work in their teens makes more sense than waiting until they are in their early twenties. They believe that partnering with educators in setting skills standards, and ensuring that VET programs are designed to help young people meet those standards, makes more sense than sitting back and waiting to see what skills young people have when they show up as job applicants. They believe that collaborating with other employers in their industry to develop a national qualifications system so they can be confident that the quality of training across firms is consistent, and that their industry sector is getting its fair share of the talent pool, makes more sense than going it alone. Above all, these employers believe it makes economic as well as social sense to invest together in building a high-quality workforce to keep their economy strong and to contribute to the education and social development of each generation of young people.

EDUCATION AND US EMPLOYER CULTURE

In contrast, US employers have virtually no history of investing in the education and training of teenagers, and consequently no reason to believe that young people could add value to their bottom line. Most US employers believe that education and training is the responsibility of high schools and especially community and technical colleges. As for socializing young people into the world of work, the United States has until recent years relied mostly on an informal youth labor market, one that operated outside our education system and consisted mostly of small retail stores and other local businesses to provide afterschool and summer employment for teens in search of spending money.

No matter their background young people who start looking for work during school to support themselves or after they finish school—whether a high school or a two- or four-year degree program—tend to face the same conundrum: if you don't have experience, you can't get a job, but if you haven't had a job, you can't get experience. Employers list "experience" in job postings not because they are biased against young people per se, but rather because they are wary of the high costs and long timeline for training new workers. They participate in a business culture that spends mega-dollars on training, but only for middle managers and executives who already have experience. US employers have a long way to go to move toward the stronger international traditions of working closely with K–12 and postsecondary institutions to ensure that school prepares young entrants for the labor market.

Real and Perceived Barriers to Employing Teens

When high school educators approach employers to seek internships or summer jobs for their students, they often encounter resistance based on concerns about federal occupational safety rules, fair labor practices, or liability issues that apply specifically to teenagers. In order to address these concerns, our colleagues on the JFF Pathways team, Charlotte Cahill and Sheila Jackson, prepared a policy brief called *Not as Hard as You Think: Engaging High School Students in Work-Based Learning*.[3] The brief includes several profiles of companies that provide internships or other forms of work experience for young people and explains how they have addressed the real or perceived barriers that are most frequently cited by other employers. As the authors conclude:

> In reality, federal and state laws and policies do not prevent high school students from participating in meaningful work experiences in professional environments. In many cases, the same guidelines and regulations associated with adult employees apply to youth under 18, making it unnecessary for employers to navigate unfamiliar policies or design new human resources processes in

order to accommodate young people. There are certain regulations based on a young person's age, the nature of the work, the hours she or he works, and the compensation he or she receives. Employers who familiarize themselves with a few main policies relevant to their sectors can easily remain in compliance while providing enriching and important career and skill development opportunities for youth that have lasting impacts on students, families, and entire communities—not to mention the employer's work and workforce.

The Disconnect Between Employers and Educators

One consequence of having so little connective tissue in the United States between the world of education and the world of work is that educators and employers have fundamentally different views about how well our schools and colleges are doing in preparing young people for employment. Study after study and poll after poll document the disconnect between the perceptions of each group about themselves in relation to the other. Polling by Gallup, for example, has shown that while 96 percent of chief academic officers at postsecondary institutions are extremely or somewhat confident in the ability of their institutions to prepare students for the workforce, only 11 percent of business leaders strongly agree that college graduates have the skills needed by employers.[4] Educators say they are doing a relatively good job preparing students for their post-education lives, and employers say they cannot find young people with the skills, knowledge, and behaviors they require for entry into their enterprises. Educators tend to believe that their job is to provide foundational skills and disciplinary knowledge during high school, with "college for all" or a postsecondary credential as the goal. Employers claim that high school and community college graduates arrive ill-prepared for the workplace and with weak skills, while educators claim that, unless and until employers demonstrate more willingness to partner in education and training designs and to open doors so that young people can gain work experience, employers won't get what they need. Even if employers were more inclined to collaborate with high schools to help prepare young people for the labor market, teachers and school leaders are generally not prepared to work with them. Most simply do not have the time or capacity to develop internships and other collaborative ventures while attending to their primary responsibilities. This is one of the reasons that, when it comes to the ubiquitous goal that students should graduate from high school "college and career ready," the latter has been an afterthought. The pathways movement is beginning to change that.

STARTING TO SHIFT: CONNECTING EMPLOYERS AND EDUCATORS

Until recently the major business organizations paid little or no attention to CTE or other forms of career-focused education.[5] Their members, mostly Fortune 500 companies, took the view that the job of the schools was to equip all students with a solid underpinning of core academic and thinking or problem-solving skills, and that technical skills would best be learned on the job. Given that most large US companies, especially those in the service sector, hire mostly people with college degrees, this was an understandable position to take. For small- and medium-size companies, however, which provide most of the jobs in the US economy, the view was somewhat different. Their expectation historically has been that schools and community colleges should be the workforce preparation system, and that they themselves should have to expend few resources on training for entry-level jobs, especially for recent graduates of community colleges or those with certifications gained in high school.

In the six years since the *Pathways* report was released, there has been a significant shift within the major national business organizations and among some leading employers in their willingness to engage with high schools and community colleges on career-related education and workforce development. Much of this has been triggered by rising concern about the skills gap. While economists may continue to debate whether the gap is real or the product of the unwillingness of employers to either raise wages or invest in training, employers in survey after survey continue to report that they cannot find workers with the skills they need to grow their business. Much of the concern focuses on middle-skill jobs, especially in the manufacturing sector, where some estimates suggest that, over the next decade, as many as

2 million jobs may go unfilled because of skill shortages.[6] One byproduct of this concern has been increasing attention to the economic performance of countries like Germany and Switzerland and the role that strong VET systems have played in enabling those countries to maintain robust manufacturing sectors and high employment rates even through the recession.

It is one thing to acknowledge that other countries have developed demonstrably more successful strategies for aligning their education system with their economic needs. It is quite another thing, and more difficult, to figure out how to adapt those policies and practices in ways that fit with our educational governance and financing structures and corporate and political cultures.

One way in which the Pathways to Prosperity Network has responded to the lessons from abroad has been our focus on building programs that span grades 9–14. This focus not only responds to the growing labor market demand for postsecondary credentials but also to the recognition that secondary-only CTE programs simply do not provide the intensity and duration of training that higher performing systems offer their students. But unless these programs are genuinely demand-driven—with employers at the table with educators from the very beginning to specify the knowledge and skills students will need to demonstrate, and to provide opportunities for students to develop and apply those skills at the workplace—simply lengthening the preparation time is unlikely to produce graduates fully ready to make a successful transition into the labor market. Hence, the continuing focus that we work on everywhere is the challenge of employer engagement.

Government Leaders and Engaging Employers

One advantage of a multistate network is that there will inevitably be a significant amount of unplanned variation in the way in which the states design and implement their career pathways systems. Although our Pathways framework is intended to provide an element of commonality across our member states and regions, in that it specifies the issues we believe each member will need to address, we fully expect each state to customize its approach based on its own institutional arrangements and political context.

One important source of variation with implications for the engagement of the employer community has been the way in which the state or region has entered the Network, and in particular who has been the lead sponsor or advocate. One thing we have learned is that when the governor or another key political leader has been the lead sponsor, it has generally been easier to bring employers to the table than when the initiative to join the Network comes primarily from K–12 leaders. The reason for this is that, by and large, governors tend to frame the argument for joining the Network in economic terms, not just in terms of what's good for young people. Our experience has been that, in states where the responsibility for recruiting employers for these kinds of activities is left to education leaders, progress is much slower.

In both Tennessee and Delaware, for example, Governors Bill Haslam and Jack Markell, respectively, have connected the dots for their constituents between the economy the state aspires to have, the gap between the skill levels of its current workforce and the skills required to attract and grow the kinds of businesses the state needs to support that economy, and the increases in educational attainment needed to produce a more skilled workforce.

Governor Haslam created a campaign around the goal of increasing the state's postsecondary attainment rate (for degrees or occupational certificates) from 32 percent to 55 percent by 2025. Then he created Pathways Tennessee, the state's strategy for getting more young people started, while in high school, on a pathway to a postsecondary credential with value in the labor market. Pathways Tennessee is followed by the Tennessee Promise of two free years of college. Similarly, Governor Markell set an attainment goal, then created the Delaware Promise and Delaware Pathways as the state's strategy to achieve that goal. In both instances, the governors enlisted their state Business Roundtable organizations as well as key industry associations as important players in the state leadership coalitions charged with implementing these strategies.[7] The fact that these two governors come from different political parties underscores the bipartisan appeal of the Pathways agenda, a rare phenomenon in our highly polarized political environment.

Employer Associations Investing in Talent

In the United States, sector-based employer associations have typically not played a significant role in helping their members address training or talent pipeline issues. Their focus has been on representing the interests of their members in the legislative arena on regulatory or taxation issues. However, as the skills gap issue has gained more prominence, this has begun to change, especially in the manufacturing sector. We got a firsthand look at the power of bringing motivated employers to the table at an early Pathways meeting in western Massachusetts.

Massachusetts manufacturing employers and Springfield Technical Community College

In late 2012, shortly after Massachusetts joined the Pathways Network, we asked the workforce board in the Springfield region to organize an initial asset mapping visit for us. The meeting brought together leaders from Springfield Technical Community College, two or three local school districts, and the leaders of the region's manufacturers association. We learned that the region was home to a significant number of high-end boutique manufacturing companies, and that these companies had come together because of their shared concern about their future workforce. The story their leaders told us was about an aging, highly skilled workforce with no successors in sight. They talked about the outdated stereotypes that most parents had about manufacturing (e.g., that factories were "dark, dirty, and dangerous" workplaces), and that these stereotypes, along with twenty years of media stories about the decline of manufacturing in the United States, meant that most young people were unaware of the very attractive career opportunities in these firms.

Consequently, the manufacturers at the table said they were willing to do whatever it took to collaborate with high schools, the community college, and the workforce board to launch a pathways program in the region to begin to build a talent pipeline. They committed to work with educators on designing a curriculum and to provide paid internships for high school students and tuition assistance to students who matriculated at the community college. As the discussion continued, the principal of West Springfield High School joined in. He said he knew nothing about manufacturing, but he knew he had plenty of perfectly capable students who were just treading water and for whom a more hands-on program—that might engage them in learning, put some money in their pockets, and get them started on a path to a postsecondary credential—could be attractive. The engineering dean from the community college was equally enthusiastic and committed to partner with the employers and the high school principal to develop dual enrollment courses that would bring the students onto the college campus while they were in high school. Consequently, a manufacturing pathway program was launched that fall at West Springfield High with sixteen students. In 2016–17 there were ninety students enrolled in the manufacturing pathway.

Arizona industry partnerships

Arizona and Delaware joined the Pathways Network together in 2015, and their pathways development strategies provide an interesting contrast. Because Delaware's participation has been government led, with an education department directly accountable to the governor, the state's CTE director and senior administrators from Del Tech were at the table from the beginning, driving the work. In Arizona, where the work has been led by a nonprofit—the Center for the Future of Arizona—and where the governmental role has been weaker, the state Pathways team decided to lead with employer associations and then work back to connect with high school and community college leaders. Based in part on our asset mapping report, the team decided to focus on two high-growth industry sectors in each of the two major population centers in the state. In the Phoenix region, the team selected energy and information technology (with a focus on cybersecurity); in the Tucson region, they chose advanced manufacturing and health/bioscience. In each case they worked through state or regional industry associations to secure strong employer support to ensure that pathways design would be demand-driven before bringing educators to the table. Although Arizona has moved more slowly than Delaware to launch new programs, given the very different political context in which the Arizona Pathways team is operating, their employer-driven strategy seems to be the right approach for that state.

Illinois Learning Exchanges

Within the Pathways Network, the most innovative state-level strategy for engaging employers is the STEM Learning Exchange program that Illinois launched in 2012.[8] The Learning Exchanges are state-sponsored, public-private partnerships that are designed to support local implementation of high-quality STEM-based programs in eight high-demand career areas: manufacturing; health science; IT; research and development; energy; finance; agriculture, food, and natural resources; and transportation, distribution, and logistics. The exchanges provide schools, teachers, and students with several different kinds of services and support, including curriculum resources, lab space and equipment, work-based learning opportunities, and professional development for teachers. Illinois used funding from the federal Race to the Top program to leverage over $8 million in private-sector resources to support the exchanges. Through a competitive process, the state awarded contracts to a lead organization to serve as the fiscal agent for each exchange. These were typically employer-led organizations. The manufacturing exchange, for example, is led by the Illinois Manufacturing Association, and the IT exchange is led by CompTIA, a leading IT association. The exchanges play an important role in aggregating resources across companies by sector and providing a "one-stop shop" for both employers and schools. At this writing, however, the future of these exchanges is unclear, given that they were initially funded for only three years, and there is a budgetary stalemate between the governor and the legislature.

The National Network

At the national level, the most promising recent development involving employer associations is the formation of the National Network of Business and Industry Associations (known now as the National Network).[9] This broad cross-section of sector-based associations, representing 75 percent of job growth projected by 2020, came together under the joint sponsorship of the ACT Foundation and Business Roundtable to address the skills gap by bringing together the worlds of work and learning. What binds these organizations across such diverse sectors as manufacturing, energy, retail, health care, construction, transportation, and IT is that they all face the challenge of finding skilled talent to fill their millions of open jobs. The National Network set for itself the following areas of focus:

- setting national standards for industry credentials
- identifying cross-sector knowledge, skills, and abilities to make educational programming more effective and efficient
- expanding work-based learning
- changing HR practices so employers "hire for competency"
- creating more learning pathways that yield employment outcomes

The National Network's first two publications—a work and learn guidebook with case studies of industry-led partnerships, and a common employability skills framework agreed to by its members—have gained significant traction in the workforce field, as has its advocacy for a competency-based credentialing system. Because the National Network now operates under the umbrella of Business Roundtable, its ability to advance its skills and credentialing agenda within the Fortune 500 employer community is likely to grow. We hope to forge a strong connection between our Pathways Network and the National Network to enable a more coordinated effort to address simultaneously both sides of the skills gap problem—demand as well as supply.

Leading Corporate Exemplars

While the problem of scale can be addressed only through the mobilization of industry associations representing large numbers of employers, especially the small- and medium-size companies that represent the bulk of present and projected job openings, large employers can play an important role in providing powerful, highly visible examples of how companies can act in their own economic self-interest by engaging with education institutions to address their long-term talent needs. Big companies do this in several different ways. Some major global leaders, most notably IBM and SAP, have focused on the development of new school models that provide young people with the knowledge and skills needed to get started in careers in their sector and, in the case of IBM, that commit to put graduates at the front of the hiring queue. Other companies, most notably the Wonderful Company in California's Central Valley, described in chapter 3, have embraced a broader regional strategy, building consortia involving multiple schools, community colleges, and employers to address regional workforce needs. Still others, most notably JPMorgan Chase, have used their philanthropic arm to advance the career pathways agenda more broadly. The following are short descriptions of what each of these corporate leaders has done:

- **IBM** has long been a leader in K–12 reform. In 2011, in partnership with the New York City Department of Education and the City University of New York, IBM launched P-TECH, Pathways in Technology Early College High School. The school is designed to span grades 9–14 and to enable students to graduate with both a high school diploma and an associate's degree in either electromechanical engineering technology or computer information systems. In addition to providing the school with substantial curriculum and professional development supports and connecting students to tutors from the company, IBM promises to place successful graduates first in line for appropriate openings. There are now six additional schools modeled on P-TECH in New York City, five in Chicago, thirty-two opened or in planning elsewhere in New York State, and another half-dozen in Rhode Island and Colorado.

- **SAP**, a German software and business solutions company, has followed IBM's example and sponsored small, technology-focused high schools in New York, Boston, Oakland, and Vancouver. As with IBM, it has provided not only technology and other supports to the school, but mentors and internship opportunities for all participating students.

- **JPMorgan Chase** launched a $75 million initiative in 2015, New Skills for Youth, $35 million of which supported a competition among the states to develop career pathways systems very similar in design to those we've been advancing through the Pathways Network. Forty-four states applied for funding, twenty-five were given planning grants, and ultimately ten were selected, including Pathways Network members Delaware, Massachusetts, and Tennessee. In addition to these state-level grants, Chase is also supporting major career pathways investments in Detroit, Denver, and New York, where the company is—in addition to its philanthropic investments—launching a pathway initiative with Guttman Community College focused on getting more young New Yorkers launched on careers in the financial services industry.[10]

European Company Exemplars

One very promising development in the last few years had been the attempt on the part of European-based companies operating in the United States to adapt their home country education and training practices to the US education setting:

- **Siemens and Daetwyler** were part of a set of German and Swiss companies that, in 1995 in Charlotte, North Carolina, came together with Central Piedmont Community College to establish Apprenticeship 2000. Twenty years later, Apprenticeship 2000 continues to offer apprenticeship opportunities to students in ten regional school districts in such manufacturing fields as mechatronics, tool and dye making, and CNC machining. While the scale of these programs remains small, students enroll in the program as high school seniors and graduate four years later from the community college with an associate's degree, a journeyman's card, federal and state certification, and a job in the host company.
- **Volkswagen** opened a major plant in the Chattanooga region of Tennessee in 2011. The company partnered with Chattanooga State Community College to create a three-year mechatronics program leading to an associate's degree in engineering systems technology, and a mechatronics certification from Volkswagen that is good worldwide. The program consists of five semesters of coursework and three semesters of paid work experience at Volkswagen, with a conditional promise of a job upon graduation.
- **Zurich Insurance** launched the first US apprenticeship program in the insurance industry, in partnership with William Rainey Harper College

in Illinois. Zurich Insurance is one of several Swiss companies operating in the United States that signed a memorandum of agreement with the US government to expand its training programs here. The Zurich program focuses on underwriting and claims. Graduates of this program will receive an associate's degree in business administration.

These program examples are small-scale and represent an apprenticeship model that blends work and learning and serves students in their late teens, making them much closer in structure to the European youth apprenticeship model than to the typical US apprenticeship program, which serves students in their mid- to late twenties and is mostly disconnected from education.

THE CRITICAL IMPORTANCE OF INTERMEDIARY ORGANIZATIONS

When we talk about the leadership role employers play in strong vocational systems outside the United States, that role is organized and supported by the industry-sector associations to which employers belong. These associations function as intermediary organizations, sitting between individual companies on the one hand and schools and young people on the other. They work with companies to provide guidance on the kinds of assignments and tasks young people can be asked to take on at the workplace, and to ensure that companies are providing the kind of coaching and support young people need in order to successfully carry out those assignments. In the dual-system countries like Switzerland, the industry associations work closely with educators to specify the competencies that young people are expected to develop at the workplace over a three- or four-year period; provide curriculum support and trained assessors to evaluate student performance against those standards; and engage in a continuous review and improvement cycle with educators to ensure that programs are kept current with changes in the industry. Without the support these associations provide, it would be virtually impossible for most Swiss or German or Austrian employers to participate in the dual system, as well over 90 percent of companies in these countries are small and would not have the capacity to do this on their own.

In the American examples described in this chapter, industry associations like the members of the National Network or those leading the Illinois Learning Exchanges are playing a much more modest role than their counterparts in Europe; for example, they are not being asked to provide even short-term internships for most of the students in the regions they serve. This is not to diminish the important contributions they make in mobilizing employer resources to help the schools strengthen career preparation, but rather to acknowledge that, if the goal is to provide most students with a well-structured workplace learning experience while they are in high school, it will take a much different level of commitment and organizational capacity than we have previously expected of such associations.

Types of Intermediaries

Because effective intermediary organizations are an essential lever in our Pathways framework, the search for one or more such organizations is a focal point in the asset mapping process in every region we work in. As our work has developed, we have come to differentiate among types of intermediaries and their various roles and functions. The functions carried out by intermediaries generally fit within two broad categories.

Convener intermediaries

The first is a convening role that involves guiding the work of a regional steering committee or other leadership entity, including:

- setting the agenda and holding the vision for pathways in the region;
- developing and convening subgroups to develop or carry out specific elements of the Pathways work;
- identifying functions, which may then be distributed to other entities, that are needed within a regional hub;
- evaluating the outcomes of the work and holding others accountable to identified metrics; and
- building public support for the work by educating the general public and policy makers about the benefits of creating career pathways and providing work-based learning to youth.

In the Pathways to Prosperity Network we have several examples of strong organizations that carry out this set of intermediary functions. In the Twin Cities, for example, it is the regional United Way that plays this role. It is a powerful, well-staffed organization that is both funder and convener and plays a strong operational role as well. By contrast, in Arizona the convening intermediary is a small, self-described "think and do tank" housed within Arizona State University, the aforementioned Center for the Future of Arizona. Led by a highly respected former ASU president, it is seen as a nonpartisan broker in an often contentious political environment. A third example is the role that Columbus State Community College plays in Central Ohio, where it is both operator and convener.[11]

Intermediaries for work-based learning

The second set of intermediary functions is focused on developing career readiness experiences for youth (e.g., work-based learning opportunities) and engaging employers and industry to sponsor them, including:

- analyzing regional labor market information as preparation for conducting other functions;
- recruiting high-level, visible business champions;
- brokering and aggregating opportunities for career awareness, exploration, and immersion activities, including work-based learning;
- assessing needs for support from schools and employers and brokering agreements between partners, including executing contracts and informal agreements between employers and schools;
- developing and designing workplace experiences (e.g., job shadows, virtual projects, internships, apprenticeships);
- providing young people with workplace orientations and general training in the basics of a career area (including work-readiness certifications);
- developing work-based learning experiences and carrying out assessments in partnership with educators; and
- reaching out to and partnering with community-based organizations.

The structure of intermediaries may vary considerably depending on state and regional needs and available resources. A single organization may take on the entire intermediary role, or the intermediary functions may be spread across multiple organizations. For example, a regional steering committee could play the convening role, while an employer association could broker work-based learning opportunities. Intermediaries can be organized by region and serve employers in multiple fields, and their responsibilities usually go beyond providing young people with workplace learning experiences to include training services for adults, regional economic development, business planning, and even marketing. Existing organizations that could carry out intermediary functions include a state or region's workforce board, other workforce training organizations, chambers of commerce, sectoral or professional organizations, and community-based organizations. Organizations carrying out intermediary functions are most commonly private, nonprofit entities that have a track record of representing and partnering with employers and government bodies. Intermediaries may also be organized by economic sector—as is often the case with trade and professional associations—with each providing expertise within a range of related occupations.

For purposes of engaging employers as partners with schools in the provision of workplace learning opportunities, regions need organizations that are employer-facing and are staffed to help both schools and employers do their part to ensure that the workplace experiences are designed to support student learning and growth. Across our Network, there are various types of organizations that take on this role, but typically the function we are describing—brokering internships or other extended workplace learning opportunities for in-school youth—is not central to the organization's mission.

Intermediaries are needed both to play the convening, organizing, and planning roles, as described in the examples of the Center for the Future of Arizona and the United Way in the Twin Cities, and to scaffold and support the development of high-quality internships, as in the example of the Boston Private Industry Council that follows. In some regions, a single organization takes on both sets of intermediary functions, but more typically these are handled separately.

The Boston Private Industry Council

The most outstanding and impressive exception to this generalization is the Boston Private Industry Council, widely known as the PIC.[12] The PIC defines itself as having two roles. It is Boston's workforce board and the city's school-to-career intermediary. The PIC was created in the late 1970s in response to federal workforce legislation aimed at increasing employer involvement in the workforce system, but from the outset it defined a much broader policy-setting role for itself than simply administering federal workforce funds. For one thing, it was set up as an independent nonprofit, not as a city agency. This provided the PIC with the flexibility to seek funding from other public and private sources and not be constrained by the requirements of the federal authorizing legislation.

Because the major civic issue in Boston in the late 70s was the continuing turmoil surrounding the implementation of a highly contentious federal court order to desegregate the Boston Public Schools, the PIC's first board chair, William Edgerly, saw the PIC as a potential vehicle to help defuse community unrest by providing access to job training and employment for young people whose education had been substantially disrupted. Consequently, in 1981, Edgerly and a small group of fellow corporate leaders negotiated an agreement, known as the Boston Compact, with a new school superintendent to trade improved access to entry-level jobs in the downtown economy for improved academic performance in the city's high schools. What gave the Compact teeth was the commitment to annual measurable goals on both sides, and to public reporting on progress. On the school side, the goals focused on improved test scores in reading and math, improved attendance rates, and reduced dropout rates. On the business side, the goals focused on increases in private-sector summer jobs, afterschool jobs, and most important, jobs for high school graduates. The PIC was designated as the organization responsible for carrying out the business community's side of the bargain, which necessitated hiring a set of career specialists who would be deployed in Boston's high schools to be responsible for matching students and jobs.

The infrastructure built thirty-five years ago at the PIC to support the jobs side of the Boston Compact continues in place to this day. In summer 2016, the PIC placed over 3,700 Boston high school students in private-sector paid internships, largely due to the work of the PIC career specialists in each high school and the related staff responsible for managing portfolios of companies. The PIC has two kinds of staff positions that go a long way toward supporting employers in matching their needs with the skill and talent of a young person. The staff are career specialists who have a caseload of one or more high schools, know the students, and help to match them with jobs; and account managers who are responsible for signing up a quota of employers, working sector by sector to construct job descriptions, and, during the summer, troubleshooting and managing employer/student relationships as needed.

Although the PIC is clearly an outlier among workforce boards nationally in its focus on in-school youth, all such boards in Massachusetts benefit from a line item in the state budget called "connecting activities." This program provides funding through the Department of Elementary and Secondary Education to the workforce boards to support the provision of internships and other work-based learning opportunities for in-school youth. Given that nearly all federal workforce funding is targeted to adults and out-of-school youth, without this state appropriation it is unlikely that workforce boards outside of Boston would have the resources to engage at all with high school students.

*   *   *   *   *

The reason we consider employers and intermediaries in the same chapter is to underscore the interdependence of these two Pathways levers. Simply put, the lesson from Switzerland and other countries with strong VET systems is that most companies would be unable or unwilling to engage with schools, or to provide structured workplace learning opportunities for students, without the support of well-resourced intermediary organizations.

CHAPTER 7

POLICIES THAT
SUPPORT PATHWAYS

Building systems of grade 9–14 pathways that launch young people into family-supporting careers in high-growth fields requires enormous effort on the part of countless players in each state or region—K–12 educators, community college leaders, employers, intermediaries, funders, and of course students themselves. There is one other group of people whose work is essential—policy makers. Effective public policies and funding streams, along with strong leadership, play a critical role in bringing together the diverse coalitions of stakeholders needed to succeed. This includes policies and policy makers at all levels that affect education and workforce development in states and regions; the focus here is policies enacted by state governments, including legislation and executive orders, as well as policies set by state education agencies and governing boards.

Good policies can provide incentives for education institutions, intermediaries, and employers to work together to support pathways development. They can promote collaboration across divides between secondary and postsecondary education and between education and workforce development. They can also ensure a flow of flexible and dependable funding for education-to-career pathways despite the funds coming from disparate sources. It is worth noting that good policy of course cannot *ensure* local capacity or quality implementation, but it can *enable* both. Meanwhile, policies that are outdated, overly prescriptive, or made without concern for unintended consequences can act as barriers to progress. In addition, the absence of relevant policy—what some call *policy neutrality*—can allow for grassroots innovation, but the state must ultimately harness local efforts to put systemic change in place.[1]

This chapter addresses one lever of the Pathways framework: effective leadership and enabling state policies. As we have discussed, the Pathways framework identifies a series of five levers. Policy has major implications for the implementation of the other four. If policy leaders do not come together across education, labor, commerce, and workforce, policies may work at cross purposes to support similar goals. If policy does not allow funding streams to be blended across grades 9 through 14, regional partnerships are left to figure out workarounds one by one. In the Pathways policy set, policies that support the grade 9–14 career pathways lever are the best developed, largely because of JFF's work since 2002 to support the Early College High School Initiative and to advise states, regions, and districts on implementation of dual enrollment. Policies related to the other three levers are less developed. This chapter begins with a look at the governance and leadership arrangements that enable policy in the first place. It ends with some examples of how states fund pathways development. For each lever, we highlight a selection of state efforts that are helping to secure pathways systems, but also speculate about policies that are not currently in place but might be desirable to better link intermediaries, employers, and industry groups with education institutions.[2]

Several additional observations provide important context for this discussion. First, no single state in the Pathways Network has the ideal policy set, but each brings to the table policies that make possible critical aspects of the Pathways design. Second, even as regions and cities have joined the Network as members on their own without their states, they have put pressure on state agencies and employer leadership groups to enact supportive policies and remove barriers to implementation. This up-from-the-field policy advocacy provides a window into what kinds of policies are proving most helpful. Third, while federal policy plays only a modest role in the funding and design of career-focused pathways, federal agency initiatives can push policy in important directions. Of note and well aligned with the Pathways framework is Youth CareerConnect (YCC), a $100 million Department of

Labor investment funded in 2014 and designed to integrate academic and career-focused learning to increase students' access to postsecondary education and employment in in-demand industries. A number of states and organizations, including JFF, used these funds to put in place their initial Pathways designs.

And finally, a president can use the bully pulpit to reinforce policy priorities as President Obama did in announcing Youth CareerConnect and similar initiatives. Indeed, he spoke frequently of the challenges young people face in getting a first job, and his administration made numerous investments beyond YCC with the goal of helping young people enter the labor market. In his 2016 State of the Union address, Obama said, not for the first time, "We need to do everything we can to make sure America's young people get the opportunity to earn the skills and a work ethic that come with a job. It's important for their future, and for America's." Although the funds were never appropriated, soon after the State of the Union, the White House proposed a $6 billion set of grant opportunities to help youth "gain the work experience, skills, and networks" they need to get entry-level jobs.

CROSS-AGENCY STATE LEADERSHIP TEAMS

Building a statewide system of high-quality career pathways for all young people begins at the state level with a commitment to a multifaceted and long-term state investment. Assembling a state-level team to do the work is a critical first step and a sign of this commitment. Because the goal is better preparing the next generation of employees to fuel state economies, as well as raising high school and postsecondary completion rates, educators alone cannot successfully lead the team. Whether the Pathways initiative is introduced by the governor, a state agency, a legislative committee, or concerned business leaders, a cross-agency leadership team must be in place to lead and support the work. The design, planning, and decision making should include state agencies responsible for economic development, commerce, workforce and labor, K–12 and higher education, and nonprofit and industry-sector leaders.

GOVERNANCE ARRANGEMENTS

As the Pathways Network has developed, we have seen growing variation in the state agency or entity that initiates contact with the Pathways team and serves as the convening entity. State education agencies (SEAs) were the first to reach out to us. We have learned, however, that if the SEA is the convener, it can be a challenge to move from a K–12 mindset to a strategy that builds backward from the state's labor market priorities and regional economic development plans. District boundaries generally are more limited than a labor shed, and in the districts' view their responsibilities end with each student cohort's high school graduation. A noneducation convening agency can more easily adopt a mindset where the end goal is productive employment for youth, requiring collaboration with a range of actors and entities.

Along with SEAs, pathways states now have lead conveners in departments of commerce (Indiana), departments of higher education (Massachusetts), the governor's office (Delaware), and state-level nonprofit organizations (California, Illinois, Texas, and Arizona). State-level nonprofits can be major assets as conveners if they are in an established public-private partnership with a state entity. The nonprofit can move nimbly, take risks, and speak with an outsider policy advocacy voice, while the state can muster resources and utilize its structure for interacting with local education agencies to systematize pathways. Regional nonprofit entities can also surface policy challenges and reach up to the state to advocate for policy changes, but they generally have less clout than statewide nonprofits.

Over the past five years, cross-agency policy-making arrangements have not always been stable. Governors and commissioners change, and budgets fluctuate. Pathways membership has survived in most but not all cases, and in some instances, states have gone "on sabbatical" during transitions and later reengaged. Those states with stability, especially in relation to the convening person or agency, have had more linear pathways development, though linear development is not the only way the work moves forward. Perhaps the two best examples of the power of cross-agency state leadership are Tennessee and Delaware, both of which have had the advantage of two-term governors who used their bully pulpit to promote and support major statewide efforts under the Pathways rubric. California and Texas present excellent examples of nonprofits working in informal partnerships with state agencies to convene leadership teams.

Program and State Showcase

Tennessee

Tennessee's membership in the Pathways Network was preceded by the prior governor's recognition that his state needed a better-educated workforce. Governor Bill Haslam built on former Governor Phil Bredesen's Complete College Tennessee Act to establish Drive to 55, an umbrella for an array of state initiatives that aim to increase postsecondary attainment, including the Tennessee Promise of two free years of postsecondary education. Pathways Tennessee, the state's grade 9–14 initiative, fit well as the front end of a multifaceted strategy to address the goal of increasing Tennessee's postsecondary attainment rate to 55 percent by 2025.

The Tennessee Department of Education leads the Pathways work, staffs and convenes a Pathways state planning team comprising leadership from the Department of Labor and Workforce Development, the Tennessee Higher Education Commission, the Tennessee Board of Regents, the Governor's Office, the Tennessee State Board of Education, the Department of Economic and Community Development, the Tennessee Independent Colleges and Universities Association, and SCORE (State Collaborative on Reforming Education). There is also an office of Postsecondary Coordination and Alignment. Each member integrates the Pathways work into organizational goals and communications, including but not limited to advocacy, funding, convenings, data sharing, and additional technical assistance needed to develop sustainable pathways statewide. Pathways Tennessee has been on a steady trajectory for five years, adding new regions each year until the state was fully covered, with a regional Pathways team, a funded intermediary, and consistent guidance and support from the state CTE office and staff.

Delaware

A member of the Network since 2014, this small state has moved rapidly, with now former Governor Jack Markell as leader, to implement pathways across the state. Two years into the work, six thousand students are enrolled in pathways across thirty-six schools.[3] In January 2015, Governor Markell created the Delaware Promise, which established a vision for education and workforce development. To support this goal, Governor Markell convened a state leadership team that has led the Delaware Pathways work over the last three years. The leadership team includes representatives from the Governor's Office, the Delaware Department of Education, the Delaware Department of Labor, Delaware Works, the Delaware Economic Development Office, Delaware Technical Community College, United Way of Delaware, the Delaware Business Roundtable Education Committee, and the Rodel Foundation of Delaware, a longtime partner in improving education outcomes in the state that provides critical support for the initiative. In August 2016, Governor Markell signed executive order 61, which established a permanent cross-agency Delaware Pathways Steering Committee. The steering committee—composed of the heads of the agencies represented on the leadership team and leaders from the state's business and nonprofit communities—is charged with advising the governor on Pathways priorities and guiding the leadership team's work.

Linked Learning and California Pathways Trust

In California, the Pathways effort began as a partnership among the James Irvine Foundation, the California Senate President, and the California Department of Education. The Linked Learning Alliance, a nonprofit advocacy group put in place by the Irvine Foundation to advocate for the expansion of the Linked Learning approach, is the lead convener working in an informal public-private partnership with three state agencies. This group has led the work at the state level, managing through transitions and rough spots. In 2014, using the state budget process, the senate president transformed the Linked Learning approach into a major statewide career pathways initiative and funding stream using the Pathways to Prosperity framework. (The appropriation for the Career Pathways Trust is described in the funding section of this chapter.) Today, the Linked Learning Alliance is a broad-based statewide coalition of education, industry, and community organizations, and functions both as a partner to the state and an outside organization that uses its own steering committee to modify and move the state's pathways agenda.

Educate Texas

Founded in 2004 as the Texas High School Project (THSP), Educate Texas is a public-private initiative of the Communities Foundation of Texas. With startup funding from the Bill & Melinda Gates Foundation to serve as an early college intermediary, Educate Texas has long been a creative force in the state, working with the Texas Education Agency and the Texas Higher Education Coordinating Board to increase the postsecondary success of low-income students and low performing schools. Working with partners, Educate Texas has opened or redesigned hundreds of schools, including early college high schools, T-STEM academies, and more recently CTE and career-focused early colleges. Educate Texas was instrumental in the state joining the Pathways Network, and, thanks to its strong relationships with the legislature and government agencies, put together a cross-sector partnership including the Texas Education Agency, Texas Higher Education Coordinating Board, Texas Workforce Commission, Office of the Governor, and the Texas legislature. Today, Texas is home to 198 early college high schools, including 41 newly designated campuses. The increasing number of early colleges with a career focus can be directly tied to the strong and consistent partnership between Educate Texas and the state.

Massachusetts

Massachusetts illustrates the twists and turns of state-level Pathways leadership—that is, what can happen when governors turn over and secretariats change. In Massachusetts, Pathways was launched in 2012 by the secretary of education, who raised private funds for the membership fee. He engaged the secretaries of labor and workforce development and housing and economic development, hired a director of education and workforce development to coordinate across all three secretariats, and began the Pathways initiative by pulling in interested community college presidents. In its second year, with a different secretary of education in place, the state team ceased meeting. Massachusetts shifted its Pathways initiative to the Office of College and Career Readiness, a unit within the Department of Elementary and Secondary Education (ESE) that works collaboratively with the Department of Higher Education. To its credit, ESE provided substantial support to grassroots early college career-focused efforts. Under Governor Charlie Baker, elected in 2014, the state is active again and moving forward rapidly with career-focused pathways through the New Skills for Youth initiative and an investment in career-focused early colleges. A state-level team has been reconstituted under the rubric of High Quality Career Pathways to bring policy coherence to the new strands of work, and again community college presidents are expressing their strong interest in leading early college development. Thus, Massachusetts leaders are now crafting policy built on national best practice as well as from what has been a locally driven career pathways movement.

LEVER I: GRADES 9–14 PATHWAYS

Career-Focused Dual Enrollment Policies

The best-developed policies enabling the accelerated grade 9–14 model embraced by the Pathways Network encourage and support high school students to prepare for and take college courses at no cost. The foundation of such policies is dual enrollment—the mechanism that permits replacement of high school requirements with college courses. Drawing on over fifteen years of experience with early college high schools, JFF has refined a dual enrollment policy set and seen it implemented in a number of states. States with expanded dual enrollment opportunities have seen that, if open to a wide range of students, such programs can increase student motivation to complete high school, enroll in and complete a postsecondary credential, and save education dollars for both families and the state.

Dual enrollment was the foundation policy for the original early college design. The grade 9–14 Pathways model makes two key additions to the original approach: all pathways are career focused and thus include CTE and other applied learning, and all aim for students to complete an associate's degree with currency in the labor market. The original early college model was geared strongly toward a liberal arts bachelor's, rather than an associate's. Our perspective is that armed with a career-focused associate's degree, a young person can enter the labor market, then decide whether she or he wants to pursue additional education. If a student is lucky enough to work for a company that provides tuition benefits—as many companies do—she may be able to go on to a further degree debt-free. Or, armed with a marketable two-year degree, a young person can at least support herself through further education.

Strong dual enrollment policies to support career-focused pathways include programs that are:

- financed so that there are no tuition costs for students—secondary and postsecondary partners are held harmless (e.g., per-pupil enrollment funding is maintained for both) or share costs equitably with additional state support;
- structured so that college-level courses, both CTE and general education, taught to high school students are counted simultaneously for high school credit toward graduation as well as for postsecondary nonelective credit;
- enable students to advance into college-level work when they are ready, based on subject-/course-specific criteria defined by colleges rather than overall GPA or test scores;
- integrate technical instruction and curricula with the required foundation of college-ready courses, including college-prep math and science needed for technical careers;
- provide "endorsements" and honors options for high achievement and completion of a career-focused major paralleling recognition for AP and IB course work; and

- designed with employer input using real-time labor market information and other data sources to ensure job projections are considered in curriculum design and applied learning experiences.

Policy Challenges

Dual enrollment policies must enable the movement of students, credits, faculty, and funding across the secondary and postsecondary education systems. Without some way for costs to be shared for college tuition and other items, early college career pathways cannot reach any scale. States have multiple strategies and arrangements for paying for dual enrollment—complex cost sharing arrangements, transfers from district per-pupil spending to colleges for tuition, and simple stipulations that tuition must be waived under specific circumstances. Whatever the arrangement, funding for dual enrollment puts a strain on budgets, and hence on incentives for cooperation. While JFF's dual enrollment advice is to hold high schools and community colleges harmless in regard to funding, in truth, states struggle to set up equitable ways to fund dual enrollment in the short term despite evidence that replacing high school courses with college courses and accelerating student accumulation of college credits results in long-term savings. It remains to be seen how or if the trend toward free community college impacts policy and practice regarding free college courses for high school students.

A second challenge comes from the significant differences between the structures of K–12 and higher education systems. Everything from semester schedules to credits versus Carnegie units to problems of incompatible data platforms must be negotiated. In addition, MOUs between high school and postsecondary partners must address such policy issues as how students qualify, whether credit transfers throughout a system, and whether students need to be informed of the program. In addition, some states still have Tech Prep, a program established in 1990 in the federal Carl Perkins Act that provided postsecondary credit for CTE high school students. Sometimes called a 2 + 2 program or articulated credit, Tech Prep allows students to take postsecondary CTE courses in high school, but credit is awarded *only* when the student enrolls at the provider community college, and is not transferable. Thus, students do not get the motivation that comes with true college credit attainment in the high school grades; furthermore, they may not want to participate knowing that the credit will be lost if they do not enroll in the provider institution.

Program and State Showcase

All Pathways states except Massachusetts and New York currently have dual enrollment policies in statute that can support grade 9–14 pathways. Massachusetts funds dual enrollment through a fluctuating line item in the state budget; conditions for the use of these limited funds are set by the board of higher education.[4] While New York does not have a state policy, in New York City dual enrollment is widely available through CUNY's College Now program. The SUNY system has a special tuition waiver option for P-TECHs. In other states, legislation spells out funding arrangements, student qualifications for access, limits on the number and selection of courses, quality standards, and how dual enrollment is counted in the state's accountability system, if at all. The following are several innovations in dual enrollment policy revision in which CTE has featured prominently.

Comprehensive dual enrollment policy overhaul

Most dual enrollment policies were designed in the 1980s and 90s to allow gifted and talented students to get a head start on college by opting to skip some high school courses and replace them with college courses. Programs often charged students tuition, and had stringent access requirements. As dual enrollment became a strategy for scaffolding low-income young people and those at risk of not completing a postsecondary credential into college, policy changes were needed. Now most states cast a wider net in dual enrollment programs, and a recent trend is to include postsecondary CTE courses, not just general education requirements, in dual enrollment policies.

A second trend is to reward students who complete CTE sequences and certifications with special designations on their diplomas. Many of these CTE endorsements, honors, or seals combine secondary and postsecondary offerings. Examples include North Carolina (CTE seal), Ohio and Texas (CTE or career area endorsements), and Florida and Louisiana (industry certification). Ohio, Florida, Indiana, and several other states are offering honors-type designations for CTE certifications as in North Carolina. This trend appears to be spreading to additional states. Texas requires special mention. In 2006, the Texas Education Agency created an early college designation for which early colleges could apply. Successful applicants for the designation get a planning period, technical assistance, and other supports from the state. Texas's early colleges are designed so that at-risk students can earn up to an associate's degree concurrent with their high school diploma at no cost and with additional supports from the state. When House Bill 5 was passed by the Texas legislature in 2013, it placed an emphasis on more career-focused pathways to graduation. One result was the establishment of designated CTE early college high schools that provide industry certifications and credits through an associate's degree with an aim of meeting the state's need for highly skilled technical workers.

Standards revision

An additional development of the last five years is the updating of CTE standards, elimination of outmoded programs, and modernization of existing ones. In some fields—IT, advanced manufacturing, health care, culinary arts—the challenge was to keep up with new technological developments as well as to create pathways for entirely new careers (e.g., health informatics and data analytics). In 2013, Advance CTE set the stage for revision by bringing together forty-four states to create a Common Career Technical Core.[5] Over the next several years, myriad states revised their standards and sent them to a board of education, regents, or higher education for approval. The goal of Tennessee's revision is similar to others: "to ensure that all new courses promoted by the department were rigorous, relevant, and student-focused." Tennessee is also developing low-stakes and high-stakes course assessments to ensure that students are achieving marked growth in targeted skills attainment.[6]

Two states' revision of CTE are particularly bold. On the funding and structure side, Ohio has streamlined and overhauled what was an overly complicated dual enrollment policy. Problems included multiple and confusing options for college course taking and a funding burden on high schools that resulted in disincentives for districts to participate. Louisiana has created a totally different way for eleventh and twelfth graders to go to school to earn CTE certifications.

College Credit Plus

College Credit Plus, a new policy proposed by the Ohio Board of Regents and enacted by the Ohio legislature, consolidates and reframes fragmented and underutilized approaches to dual credit into a single policy, and might be called a second-generation policy.[7] The law requires all school districts, including vocational centers, and public higher education institutions to make opportunities available at no cost to low-income students. Each high school must offer two model pathways with a partnering college— one pathway requiring fifteen transcripted credits and the other requiring thirty—including all courses that apply to at least one degree or professional certification offered at the college. College Credit Plus also sets a floor and ceiling for the costs that higher education institutions can charge school districts for dual enrollment. The Ohio Department of Education deducts the negotiated tuition costs from the school district's budget. To meet the need, the state provided scholarships for high school teachers to gain credentials to teach college courses.

Louisiana's Jump Start

One particularly interesting experiment to watch is Louisiana's Jump Start, a new CTE program that has fully replaced CTE concentrations. Jump Start restructures the eleventh and twelfth grades for students choosing a career diploma. Participating high school students are provided more time in the school day and year to achieve industry certificates or college credentials in addition to their high school diplomas. Jump Start credentials are state-approved.[8] The program combines a number of the positive policy developments underlying career pathways: schools get a premium for mounting programs in high-demand sectors, employers are providing embedded work experiences, the career diploma has the same weight as an academic honors diploma for university-bound students, and regional teams advise on and select the certifications in response to economic needs.[9]

LEVER II: CAREER AWARENESS, EXPOSURE, AND WORK-BASED LEARNING

Student Learning Plans and School Counseling

Career advising, exposure to careers, and work-based learning are critical to the success of pathways and to the success of young people. But in general, none of these is an area for state policy. If these activities are implemented at all—as we call for in the Pathways framework—they are district-designed and happen at the district level. Policy marginally addresses some aspects of career advising through student learning plans (SLPs), but not at all career exposure or work-based learning. Twenty-three states now require SLPs, some only for special populations (gifted and talented, English language learners, special education, and CTE).[10]

Unfortunately, required SLPs all too often become compliance exercises. The common challenge is unworkably high ratios of counselors to students, with many counselors barely able to meet the demand for college application support while attending to various students' health and family emergencies, let alone to develop and delve into individualized career advising activities. Nonetheless, SLPs can provide valuable building blocks for career preparation, including informing students about work-based learning opportunities and courses that teach about career fields and pathways.[11] *Personal Opportunity Plans*, a brief produced by Educators for Social Responsibility for the Nellie Mae Education Foundation, develops a comprehensive vision of what a plan that moves far beyond typical counseling functions might encompass—arguing that constructing and following a meaningful life plan, including finding a calling or career, is a primary purpose of schooling.[12]

Of the Pathways states, California (grades 7–12), Texas, and Tennessee require career counseling and in Wisconsin, career planning will be required starting in the 2017–18 school year.[13] States and districts are increasingly buying or building online platforms for their school systems, making career information available in classrooms, often along with options for students to create electronic portfolios highlighting their career plans, showing samples of their academic work, and documenting other accomplishments.

Program and State Showcase

Colorado: SLPs

Among states mandating SLPs, Colorado is implementing a required Individual Career and Academic Plan (ICAP) starting in high school. More than most, ICAP puts future work at the center of students' exploration of steps beyond high school. As the ICAP website for Boulder Valley explains, "ICAPs begin with a vision of what a student would like to do in the world of work. This could mean identifying a career cluster (grouping of careers) that interests them, or a specific career, and then linking what they are interested in doing in the world of work with courses, extracurricular activities, and postsecondary plans. All districts must provide ICAP access and assistance for every student in grades 9–12 (ICAP Legislation)."[14]

Wisconsin: Academic and Career Planning

In 2013 under the rubric of Education for Employment, Wisconsin launched an Academic and Career Planning (ACP) process focused on helping students develop postsecondary and career plans. ACP incorporates a continuum of activities in four domains: self-exploration, career exploration, career planning, and management. ACP is supported by a bill passed by the state legislature that provides the Department of Public Instruction with the funding and legal authority needed for the ACP process. The state is making Career Cruising, an online career exploration platform, available to all districts in the state that want to use it as the basis for the district-level ACP process. By the 2017–18 school year, every district in the state will be required to provide

ACP services to all students in grades 6–12, though the content and structure of those services may differ from one district to the next.[15]

Texas: Career advising and counseling

With the 2015 passage of House Bill 18, Texas took a significant step toward improving the availability of high-quality college and career advising at the middle and high school levels. The legislation established an initiative to educate counselors and advisors about the range of pathways and career opportunities available to students. It requires school districts to provide seventh and eighth graders with instruction focused on preparing them for high school, college, and careers. HB 18 was intended to meet the need for increased advising capacity with the implementation of the Foundation High School program (HB 5), enacted in 2013, which created new advising and graduation pathways requirements for Texas high schools.

HB 18 is being implemented through Texas OnCourse—an initiative of the University of Texas at Austin, working in partnership with the Texas Education Agency, the Texas Workforce Commission, and the Higher Education Coordinating Board. Texas OnCourse is supporting professional development for counselors and advisors through the development of technology-enabled advising tools and professional support networks. Texas OnCourse is also creating online content modules focused on career, postsecondary, and financial aid advising for both counselors and students.

Massachusetts: SLPs

While not a policy mandate, in Massachusetts, guidance from the Department of Elementary and Secondary Education links student learning plans to other priority state initiatives, such as increasing high school graduation rates, the use of the Massachusetts Model for School Counselors, and the participation of students in career development education activities. Massachusetts created an Individual Learning Plan Guide for schools and districts that illustrates how these plans overlap with other required student plans, such as C/VTE career plans and special education transition plans.

LEVER III: EMPLOYER ENGAGEMENT

Given the challenges of the job market for young people today, the premium employers put on experience, and the body of research on the positive impact of work experiences on young people, investing in work-based learning and internships should be a high priority for states.[16] This section explores policy limitations and options to incentivize employers and educators to work together to provide scaled work-based learning. With the exception of the federal policies protecting the safety of those under age eighteen outlined here, this policy set is underdeveloped and without a research base. We think that incentives are needed for educational institutions and employers to work together. Policies are also needed to develop and support intermediaries, the lever addressed in the next section of this chapter.

Restrictions and Limitations

Federal and state laws that regulate safety and compensation of young people play a role in shaping work-based learning—especially internships and apprenticeships. Limits and protections are based on a young person's age, the nature of the work, the hours worked during the school year, and the compensation received. Federal laws pertaining to youth employment generally fall under the US Department of Labor's Wage and Hour Division, which enforces the Fair Labor Standards Act (FLSA). The FLSA outlines federally mandated provisions related to wages and overtime pay, hours worked, record keeping, and child labor. In the industries generally targeted for pathways development, there is only one common activity—operating a forklift—among the FLSA's list of seventeen "hazardous occupations" in which young people are not permitted to engage.[17] The FLSA limits the number of hours that fourteen- and fifteen-year-olds—but not sixteen- and seventeen-year-olds—may work. Additional restrictions on work hours for students under eighteen are generally a matter of state law, which varies across the country. All states have some laws pertaining to youth employment. These commonly address issues such as minimum wages, work permits, and required rest and meal periods. Where there is overlap between federal and state laws, the stricter standard applies.

The most significant policy in regard to the continuum of work-based learning experiences concerns internships. In 2010, as companies cut back on spending as a result of the fiscal crisis, the Labor Department became concerned that unpaid interns were being used as free labor. They began to enforce six federal legal criteria that employers must meet if they are not going to pay an intern.[18] Although many gray areas exist, especially in regard to nonprofit internships, for the most part unpaid interns may not replace paid employees. In general, it was affluent and well-connected young people who both got coveted internships and complained (justly in most cases) about exploitation, but the requirement that interns be paid actually serves to equalize opportunity somewhat, in that low-income young people generally work during summers and through college and so cannot afford unpaid internships. The payment requirement also militates against employment discrimination and sexual harassment without consequences, as unpaid interns are not covered by the laws that protect paid employees.

While protections and pay are, of course, a good thing, the law makes an unfortunate distinction between internships for the purpose of learning versus those that contribute to a company's bottom line. This distinction undermines the assumptions behind an internship or apprenticeship—that the young person is both learning and contributing, and that the benefits are mutual.[19] Indeed, the return-on-investment studies from Germany and Switzerland show just that—interns' contributions grow as they learn.

Employer-Targeted Policies to Incentivize Work-Based Learning

Policies to incentivize employers to provide work-based learning opportunities for in-school youth, if these opportunities exist, are largely associated with youth apprenticeship, internships, and co-op programs—the latter largely targeted to low achievers to allow them to work and finish up the minimum high school requirements for graduation. Incentives come in three forms: direct subsidies, tax credits, and special grants or contracts generally for program startup. Subsidies can either be full funding to an employer or an employer match to state- or city-paid wages. Tax credits work differently: the credits may be prorated depending on whether students work full or part time or whether young people are at risk or well prepared. Some states provide a range of organizations and businesses with tax credits for hiring at-risk young people, as a crime prevention strategy or to target populations that are chronically unemployed. With the partial exception of Massachusetts's Connecting Activities program (explained in the next section) and perhaps Louisiana's Jump Start, no state policies promote work-based learning as a routine activity embedded in all high school career preparation programs, as in the best European dual systems. Indeed, work-based learning generally is more "work" than "learning," a point of view that Pathways is trying to change.

Several other ideas that have been tried on a limited scale include structuring federal work-study funding to support skills-based internships aligned with a student's major; requiring companies that do business with state or local government to include paid internships in vendor contracts; and providing low- or no-cost training for incumbent workers in exchange for a company's agreement to provide a designated number of student internship placements.

Education-Targeted Policies to Incentivize Work-Based Learning

States and districts have few policies that directly mandate work-based learning, but guidelines and structures are in place to enable it. Among the structures that could prepare students for or provide work-based learning, and could be encoded in policy or regulation, are expanded learning time, independent study or credit for work-based learning, and career exposure or experience as a component of a mandated learning plan. Finally, most states regulate hours or days that make up the required amount of "seat time." These seat-time rules are often more flexible than they appear so that even if students are outside of school in a structured work experience, their time can be counted for the requirement.

LEVER IV: INTERMEDIARIES

Beyond direct incentives like tax credits and subsidies, states can also incentivize employers by providing infrastructure to support engagement with young people. Infrastructure support is usually provided by an intermediary organization such as a workforce development board, chamber of commerce, workforce organization, or other nonprofit entity. As discussed in chapter 6, intermediaries are organizations steered by key stakeholders working together to connect employers and educational institutions, and create bodies of knowledge and skills to serve the collective goals of the partners. While workforce intermediaries have long existed and can partner in providing work-based learning experiences for younger students, the organizational structures needed for partnering among schools, community colleges, and employers on behalf of younger students have different requirements than those whose target populations are low-skilled, underemployed, or unemployed adults. As states and regions build out regional ecosystems starting with grade 9–14 career pathways, they are beginning to develop the policy supports needed to engage workforce boards and other nonprofits in the work described here.

Organizations that undertake intermediary functions require funding, including a budget for paid staff, in order to successfully carry out the work. There are several possible avenues through which states can provide this support. States may direct additional state resources to workforce boards that are undertaking intermediary functions. States can also make use of their limited Workforce Innovation and Opportunity Act (WIOA) Youth funds to support intermediaries focused on work-based learning.

Program and State Showcase

Massachusetts

Massachusetts funds intermediary infrastructure to support work-based learning through a line item in the state budget for Connecting Activities. Connecting Activities is a Department of Elementary and Secondary Education initiative that provides funding to the local workforce boards to partner with school districts to offer work-based learning opportunities, as well as other career awareness activities, as part of students' preparation for college and career. Connecting Activities funding allows workforce boards across the state to hire or support staff members that work with schools and businesses to develop a wide range of career-related activities, including the implementation of individualized work-based learning plans for students; student preparation and worksite placement; and placement of young people in summer and afterschool employment targeted to high-growth industries.

Funding Strategies for Initiating and Structuring State and Regional Pathways Initiatives

While state leaders and regional and district implementers ultimately have to use existing and repurposed funding streams to sustain pathways, in a number of Pathways states, once the Pathways to Prosperity framework was in place, policy makers were able to use it to leverage specially designated funds from a variety of sources. Such investments of new funds served to attract valuable attention to the problem to be solved, and to launch or expand regional activity. On occasion but all too rarely, special funds were provided to gather critical information about the challenges and advantages of the designs being implemented, and to collect data.

Pathways leaders took advantage of three funding streams to get pathways under way: federal funding streams, state funds appropriated through line items in the budget or special state competitions, and philanthropic initiatives (see table 7.1 for examples).

Program and State Showcase

Tennessee

Under the Perkins Act, states can reserve 10% of their federal Perkins allocation to support new and innovative CTE opportunities. Tennessee has used these funds creatively to support targeted initiatives in selected regions. For example, the Highlands Economic Partnership in Upper Cumberland uses the funds to support career coaches in the high schools, while other sites have used the funds to staff an intermediary or to provide equipment for new career pathways.

Tennessee is also supporting regional consortia that are developing pathways with state funding. The Tennessee General Assembly appropriated $10 million in the 2014–15 fiscal year budget and again in the 2016–17 budget

TABLE 7.1   Federal, state, and philanthropic funding streams for pathways work

Public		Private
Federal funding examples	*State funding examples*	*Philanthropic funding examples*
Race to the Top	California Career Pathways Trust	The James Irvine Foundation's Linked Learning initiative
US Department of Labor's Youth CareerConnect (supports pathways development in communities in almost every Pathways state or region)	Tennessee Labor Education Alignment Program (LEAP) grants	The Joyce Foundation's Great Lakes College and Career Pathways Initiative
Carl D. Perkins Career and Technical Education Act of 2006 (Perkins IV; gives recipients the opportunity to create a reserve fund of up to 10 percent to be used for new and innovative programs)	Ohio Straight A grants program	JPMorgan Chase's $35 million New Skills for Youth competition

to fund two rounds of Labor Education Alignment Program (LEAP) grants administered through Governor Haslam's Workforce Subcabinet. The grants are intended to support the state's Drive to 55 initiative, and have been a significant source of startup funding for several Pathways Tennessee regions.

Delaware

Delaware has also made use of Perkins reserve funds as part of a broader braided funding strategy to support the Pathways work. The Delaware Department of Education has competitively awarded Perkins reserve funds to districts through innovation grants designed to drive pathways development.[20] The identification of braided funding as one of five core priorities in the Delaware Pathways strategic plan has spurred collaboration among state leaders seeking to build a sustainable funding structure for Pathways. With leadership from both the Rodel Foundation and the United Way of

Delaware, the Delaware Departments of Education and Labor, Delaware Technical Community College, and the Delaware Workforce Development Board have mapped existing funding streams and determined which can be used—and how—to support Pathways.

California

California leads the country with arguably the largest state investment on record devoted to career pathways. Over two legislative sessions the California Assembly and Senate, under the leadership of the senate president, budgeted $500 million to expand or develop regional grade 9–14 career pathways leading to employment in high-growth, high-demand sectors of the California economy. Three state agencies—the California Department of Education, the California Community College Chancellor's Office, and the California Workforce Development Board—together designed the application process for two rounds of a competitive grants program with three funding tiers: $15 million for large regional consortia, $6 million for smaller regional consortia, and $600,000 for regions just getting started.

New York

While California has made the largest state investment thus far, other grant-funded initiatives, including Tennessee's (as described earlier), are also supporting the startup and sustainability of pathways. Since 2013, in partnership with IBM, New York State has provided three rounds of P-TECH replication funding, totaling $56 million, to prepare New York high school students for high-skill jobs in technology, manufacturing, and health care. Students earn an associate's degree at no cost to their families and will be first in line for jobs with participating companies when they graduate. Although the state is no longer a Pathways Network member, New York City, where P-TECH began, recently joined as a region.

Texas

In 2016, Texas awarded $7.1 million to nineteen high schools to support the development of Innovative Academies, which employ pathways models to prepare students for employment in high-demand occupations. The funding was awarded by the Texas Education Agency, Texas Workforce Commission, and Texas Higher Education Coordinating Board as part of Governor Greg Abbott's Tri-Agency Workforce Initiative, which is focused on linking education and industry in order to promote economic development.

Private foundation funding

New Skills for Youth, the Great Lakes College and Career Pathways Initiative, and some smaller regional investments from private philanthropy exemplify a new trend from private foundations, which have been notoriously wary of CTE and career preparation for young people, preferring instead the "college for all" goal. With the promise of $2 million grants, in the spring of 2016 New Skills for Youth reviewed first-round applications from forty-four states, invited twenty-four states to apply for second-round funding, and ultimately funded ten, including three Pathways states—Delaware, Massachusetts, and Tennessee. This competition was influenced by the 2011 Pathways report as well as by a trip to Switzerland by a number of chief state school officers, including officials from the Council of Chief State School Officers (CCSSO), to study the country's VET system. Similarly, the Great Lakes competition—with sites funded in Ohio, Illinois, and Wisconsin—was inspired by the Pathways to Prosperity grade 9–14 pathways design and JFF's work to date.

Funding Design and Implementation

These special appropriations or funding opportunities required designs incorporating all five Pathways levers (grade 9–14 pathways; career awareness, exposure, and work-based learning; employer engagement; intermediaries; and policy). Even if the funding went to an SEA with a commitment to begin with high school redesign, recipients of funding were required to assemble a cross-sector regional steering committee including employers and to include work-based learning. Thus, employer needs were articulated as the goal.

While there are small differences in design and implementation requirements, the following are characteristic of the aspirations of Pathways initiatives:

- use of labor market data guiding pathways design toward high-growth, high-wage careers
- presence of a cross-sector stakeholder leadership group including workforce boards, local education agencies, colleges, businesses, and community-based partners to help develop the pathways and support students
- incorporation of dual enrollment and other acceleration mechanisms, generally with aspiration for an associate's degree or industry-recognized credential
- required work-based learning opportunities
- engaged employers
- state accountability system including career-focused indicators and success metrics
- plans for sustainability beyond the grant period

System building is difficult, long-term work and requires sustained leadership and political will. Given different starting points and tenure in the Network, inevitably some states and regions have made more progress than others. But in our view, with the help of the federal government and philanthropy, states must continue to support, expand, and sustain career pathways. These are critical for the healthy development of the nation's younger generations, for the overall health of the US economy, and to avoid the costs to society of a disaffected youth population ignored by their more prosperous elders. The heavy lift required to create such a system belongs to states and regions, and each has its own vision and plan for what needs to be done within the broad framework and levers of Pathways to Prosperity. The examples provided here of policies currently in place in Pathways states indicate that these states are making career pathways a reality, but they also suggest that there is substantial room for additional policy development.

CHAPTER 8

LOOKING FORWARD

We Are Not Alone

The previous chapters look back at how the Pathways to Prosperity Network came to be, how we have structured our work, what its members have accomplished over the last five years, and what we have learned in the process. Of course, our work builds on people and organizations already engaged in this kind of work, and we have acknowledged influences and partnerships along the way. But the *Pathways to Prosperity* report was undoubtedly a catalyst in reviving national interest in the link between schooling and employment, raising the issue of the still "forgotten half," and challenging the "college for all" mantra. Today, it is heartening that many other prominent voices have joined the call.

We have alluded to other players building and growing the pathways movement—and we think it *is* a movement. Some, like NAF and High Schools That Work, have been working at the school and district level for many more years than we have had a pathways movement. Although Advance CTE recently changed its name, it has been in the career education business since 1920. Others, like New Skills for Youth/CCSSO, the National Governors Association, and the US Chamber Foundation, are relative newcomers to the field.

We like to think that, beyond the report, the Pathways Network has had an influence in renewing and heightening interest in career pathways, and in part in defining what *career pathway* means. Advance CTE has used renewed interest in career education to push for modernization and expansion of CTE. It has also been an ally in the push to reinterpret CTE as a road to career-focused education for all. For networks of schools like NAF,

High Schools That Work, and Linked Learning, we think that Pathways is increasing the visibility of work on the ground to move it into the sights of governors and policy makers. For some national organizations, our work has helped shape their initiatives in the field. For example, we led a study tour of the Swiss VET system for members of the CCSSO task force on career readiness, an experience reflected in the emphasis it gave to the role of employers in its *Opportunities and Options* report.[1] But in all these cases, the learning has been two-way: our own work has been significantly influenced by our interactions with other leaders in the field.

In this final chapter, we look ahead to ask: What do we see as the major challenges facing our Network in its next five years? Before addressing this question, however, we want to reflect on the state of the growing career pathways movement and ask a more fundamental question: Are we and our colleagues building a career pathways *field* as well as a movement? To help address that question, we will use the "strong field framework" developed by the Bridgespan Group several years ago (table 8.1).[2]

The strong field framework has five components: shared identity, standards of practice, knowledge base, leadership and grassroots support, and funding and supporting policy. Shared identity is the overarching component or foundation for the framework. The framework asserts that without a shared identity, "individuals and organizations with similar motivations and goals may end up working in isolation or at cross purposes." Shared identity remains a challenge, but we think at least a couple of key elements of a strong field are beginning to emerge and can help us diagnose where the pathways movement stands.

BUILDING A CAREER PATHWAYS FIELD

Going back to the 2011 *Pathways* report and the policy statements that followed from CCSSO in 2014 and Advance CTE in 2016, we see evidence of a shared vision, if not yet a shared identity. Indeed, when these statements were issued, the Pathways team was pleased to see that their recommendations echoed a core principle of our Network: that all learners, not just

TABLE 8.1   The strong field framework

Shared identity:
Community aligned around a common purpose and a set of core values

Standards of practice	Knowledge base	Leadership and grassroots support	Funding and supporting policy
Codification of standards of practice Exemplary models and resources (e.g., how-to guides) Available resources to support implementation (e.g., technical assistance) Respected credentialing/ongoing professional development training for practitioners and leaders	Credible evidence that practice achieves desired outcomes Community of researchers to study and advance practice Vehicles to collect, analyze, debate, and disseminate knowledge	Influential leaders and exemplary organizations across key segments of the field (e.g., practitioners, researchers, business leaders, policy makers) Broad base of support from major constituencies	Enabling policy environment that supports and encourages model practices Organized funding streams from public, philanthropic, and corporate sources of support

Source: The Bridgespan Group, *The Strong Field Framework* (San Francisco: James Irvine Foundation, 2009).

those in CTE, need to participate in learning activities that link them to the world of work. Advance CTE's report, *Putting Learner Success First: A Shared Vision for the Future of CTE*, advocated for better career advising, access to real-world experiences linked to a career interest of a student's choice, and a seamless transition to aligned secondary and postsecondary programs of study.[3] CCSSO also recommended a system that engages all students. In *Opportunities and Options*, CCSSO emphasized that a new system must be "demand driven," with employers leading the way. To make career readiness matter to educators, the report said it needed to be incorporated into state accountability systems. Finally, the CCSSO report called out "important efforts already underway" and named the National Governors Association, the US Chamber of Commerce Foundation, Southern Regional Education Board (SREB), and Pathways to Prosperity as organizations that were already mobilizing governors, along with business, postsecondary, and intermediary organization leaders, to work with state education officials.

In our view, then, the career pathways movement meets one important test of a strong field: there is broad agreement among leaders in the field about common purpose and core values. We think as well that there is a growing consensus among "influential leaders and exemplary organizations across key segments of the field" about what needs to be done to advance the field, which is the first part of another component of the framework—leadership and grassroots support.

Grassroots support, however, we would characterize as a work in progress. One of the most frequent requests we get from our partners in the field is help with communications and messaging. Given the historical legacy of vocational education being seen as second class—a program for students not deemed "college material"—it is understandable that many parents might approach talk of career pathways with healthy skepticism. This can be true of suburban parents who want their schools to focus only on preparing their children for admission to the most selective universities, or of inner-city parents who remember all too well the days when students of color were routinely assigned to low-end vocational programs that prepared young people only for low-skill, dead-end jobs. While our Network members have encountered very little overt resistance to the concept of career pathways, they report a continuing need for help in reinforcing the message that all young people will need some postsecondary degree or credential to make their way in this increasingly challenging labor market, and that all young people would benefit from a more systematic introduction to the world of work and careers before leaving high school.

When we turn to the other components of the strong field framework, especially shared standards of practice and an agreed-upon knowledge base, it is clear that the career pathways field is still in its infancy. Organizations like NAF and ConnectEd California (the support organization for Linked Learning) and SREB's High Schools That Work have taken on the challenge of developing standards of practice within their own networks, but there is little agreement within the field as a whole about what such standards might look like. (One exception is the continuum of work-based learning, illustrated in chapter 5.) And despite the efforts over the years of the researchers associated with the National Research Center for Career and Technical Education and the Community College Research Center, the knowledge base remains thin, and policy makers and practitioners need support to collect and analyze data. These observations suggest an agenda of work not for the Pathways Network alone, but for the larger group of organizational players in the career pathways movement.

THE WORK AHEAD FOR THE PATHWAYS NETWORK

While there is no shortage of short-term needs and issues facing our members, we want to focus our attention in this final chapter on three major lingering issues: operationalizing career readiness, engaging community colleges, and mobilizing employers and their organizations. None of these issues is new, but we need to accelerate our progress on these challenges in order to produce the student outcomes we seek.

Career Readiness

Preparing young people to find decent work has to start early. As we have discussed, in the years since the *Pathways* report appeared, the "college for all" mantra has been replaced by the goal that all students should leave high school "college and career ready." This is good news on two counts. First, by introducing the importance of career readiness, it implicitly challenges the idea that college is a destination in itself, rather than a path to a career. Second, and more important, it moves us away from the old idea that the job of high schools is to prepare students for *either* college *or* career, not both. The challenge now is to move beyond rhetorical acceptance of the policy goal of all students graduating college and career ready to help communities design strategies to implement this policy on the ground.

Schools can draw upon a well-established portfolio of activities to expose young people to the world of higher education. In most urban centers, an array of nonprofit organizations offers college access programs. As students reach the last years of high school, college information and access activities intensify, with college fairs and financial aid workshops for students. When it comes to helping young people gain exposure to the world of work and careers, however, resources are limited. If we are going to move beyond rhetoric and fully embrace the goal of all students leaving high school college and career ready, we need to build a systematic year-by-year curriculum to ensure that all students are given the information, exposure, and opportunities for experiential learning to meet an agreed-upon standard of readiness. This is not a job that schools can or should be expected to do on their own. In New York City—one of our newest Network members—leaders from the mayor's office, the New York Department of Education, the City University of New York, and the New York City Partnership have come together to craft a "Compact for Career Readiness" that specifies each organization's roles and responsibilities in ensuring that all students, middle grades through community college, are provided with the career-related supports and opportunities they need to make informed choices along the path from high school to postsecondary education or training and to meaningful employment.

Community Colleges

In our view, community colleges are *the* critical institution in the development of a career pathways system in that they represent the bridge between high schools and employers.

In the US system, it is the community college that needs to play the central institutional role if the new, modernized, grade 9–14 approach to career-focused education is to become a route to opportunity and upward mobility for large numbers of young Americans. Community colleges have multiple missions and serve a very broad range of learners: young people seeking a low-cost first two years of college prior to transferring to a four-year institution; older adults, some with four-year degrees, seeking new technical skills; adults seeking basic education; workers sponsored by their companies seeking to upgrade their skills; retirees pursuing an avocational interest; and now students from accelerated grade 9–14 pathways entering with dual enrollment credit and in a career-focused program of study.

Community colleges operate under increasing financial constraints and are often described as "asked to do everything for anybody." Thus, it should not surprise us that, while many colleges are willing to revise, step up, or expand their workforce preparation options by launching a new mechatronics program or holding spots in allied health for high school students, they are constrained in doing so. It should also not surprise us that, given how few resources these institutions have to support a robust advising system, eighteen-year-olds fresh out of high school are often at a competitive disadvantage in seeking access to the high-demand technical programs compared to older adults who know how to work the system and may be entering with a bachelor's degree and work experience.

What would it take to enable an increased number of community colleges to play the central role we envision for them: to collaborate with high schools and employers in enrolling younger students in certificate and degree programs in high-growth, high-demand fields in their regional economies? In our view this will require state political and corporate leaders to come together and make the case publicly for a strategy that connects the dots between the state's economic future and its ability not only to increase educational attainment of young people, but to better align its certificate and degree programs with the demands of its regional economies. It's no accident that in Delaware and Tennessee, the two states we profile in chapter 3, strong political and corporate leaders have made the case for new or repurposed resources allocated to community colleges.

One major barrier that the early college/dual enrollment component of the grade 9–14 career pathways strategy is designed to address is the remediation hurdle. Early college students take no remedial courses, and complete requisites for entry to college while still in high school. But across the country, remediation remains a huge challenge. The problem is especially acute in mathematics, where college algebra is a gate through which very large numbers of students fail to pass. Fortunately, there are significant reforms under way in the community college world to reduce the proportion of students needing remediation. These range from limiting the use of placement tests for recent high school graduates and modularizing remedial courses so that students only need to relearn areas of weakness, to offering students the opportunity to take corequisite, credit-bearing courses with intensified support.

The most fundamental and promising reforms question the premise that all students need to pass through the algebra gateway. Led by two highly respected scholars, Anthony Bryk at the Carnegie Foundation for the Advancement of Teaching and Uri Treisman at the Charles A. Dana Center at the University of Texas at Austin, there is a growing movement to offer an array of new courses focused on quantitative reasoning, statistics, and math for STEM-focused technical fields.[5] Early implementation results are highly promising, showing dramatic increases in passing rates, and there is growing support among the leading mathematics associations for multiple mathematics pathways that are better aligned with the kinds of mathematics people actually need for career advancement and civic participation.

Employers

The single biggest challenge to the career pathways movement is how to create a more demand-driven system. With the important exception of the example provided by the Wonderful Company in central California, there is no region in which we work where we can say that the work is genuinely both demand- and mission-driven. This is not to say that there aren't regions where employers are fully engaged as partners at the table with educators, but the work of program design continues to be led primarily by educators, with employers joining in when persuaded to do so. We are enthusiastic about skills mapping, in which educators begin program design by examining the skills that employees actually use in an occupational setting and then map backward to build a curriculum and set of workplace learning experiences that will enable students to acquire those skills. This is so important because it gives employers the primary voice at the table.

As we argued in chapter 6, the challenge of persuading US employers to take the same kind of leadership role in building talent pipelines that their

European counterparts do is primarily cultural, not political or financial. Our employers simply do not have a tradition of banding together by sector to engage with educators or other training providers to address their work-force needs, and the kinds of changes taking place in the economy make this even less likely now than when we started five years ago. In an employer survey done by Accenture for the *Bridge the Gap* report cited earlier, while the vast majority of the employers surveyed said they were having difficulty filling middle-skill jobs, they were more likely to fill the vacancy with a tem-porary worker or even to leave the position vacant than to reach out to local community colleges or other training providers to respond to the problem.[6]

That said, there are at least three promising developments on the hori-zon that give us hope. The first is a growing Talent Pipeline Management (TPM) initiative launched by the US Chamber of Commerce Foundation in 2014. This initiative is focused on helping employers learn to apply supply-chain management principles to workplace talent acquisition. The Chamber Foundation is now working with employer organizations in 50 communities to spread this approach through the creation of the TPM Academy, a train-the-trainer model with curriculum and web-based tools to support local implementation.

The second promising development, described in chapter 6, is the for-mation of the National Network of Business and Industry Associations. Whether the National Network will move beyond its current interest in defining common employability skills and supporting the development of a competency-based credentialing system is an open question, but the fact that these employer associations, which represent 75 percent of US jobs, have come together to address their common talent issues is in itself extremely encouraging.

A third promising development is happening in Colorado. In 2015, the CEO of a family-owned manufacturing company in Denver took part in a ten-day study tour and institute in Zurich organized by Ursula Renold, the former director of the federal office that oversees the Swiss VET system. The CEO was part of an eight-person team representing the Denver Public Schools, as well as both local and state workforce leaders. Over the course of the ten days, he and his colleagues decided that there was no reason they couldn't adapt what they saw and admired in Switzerland, and the CEO in particular was convinced he could recruit other employers to join him in offering the same kind of dual-system apprenticeship opportunities to young people in Denver that he saw in Zurich. At this writing, a new organization, CareerWise Colorado, is up and running in Colorado just eighteen months later. Focused on creating youth apprenticeships for students in grades 11 and 12 in four sectors—IT, advanced manufacturing, business operations, and financial services—and launched with $9.5 million in grants from Bloomberg Philanthropies and JPMorgan Chase, it will provide 120 apprenticeships in 2017, with a goal of serving 20,000 students (10 percent of Colorado's young people) over the next ten years.[7] This will be the first test at scale of an employer-led, demand-driven, dual-system model in the United States. If it works, it will suggest that perhaps we have overestimated the difficulty of convincing US employers to engage with younger students at scale.

FINAL THOUGHTS

As our Swiss friend and colleague Ursula Renold keeps reminding us, it takes decades to change large-scale public systems, not a year or two or even five. For twelve years (through 2012), Renold was general director of the Swiss Federal Office for Professional Education and Technology, the office that oversees the Swiss system. She was the principal architect of important policy changes that have enabled that system to become the "gold standard" among vocational systems around the world.[8] But it wasn't always the place to learn engineering, IT, dance, and financial services—that took years of careful work with multiple stakeholder groups.

The Pathways to Prosperity Network is now five years old, and we can point to at least a couple of states and several regions where the work of building career pathways systems is well under way. We think it is important to pause and celebrate the progress to date, but we can't help but be mindful of how much work lies ahead. The clock is ticking in the United States, especially for the three million sixteen- to twenty-four-year-olds who are neither in school nor at work. They are a constant reminder to us of the importance of catching young people while they are still in school and doing whatever it takes to connect them to the work world and to postsecondary education before we lose them. Keeping these young people, and the recognition of the lost human potential they represent, in front of us can't help but create a sense of urgency in our work—urgency that must be balanced by the understanding that changing systems is a long-term process requiring patient and persistent commitment.

This work is not for the faint of heart, which is why we so admire the hundreds of colleagues working throughout the cities, regions, and states in the Pathways Network to whom we dedicate this book. They are working to build opportunity structures for young people to ensure that our economy remains vibrant, and that demography need not be destiny.

NOTES

Introduction

1. National Assessment of Career and Technical Education, *US Department of Education: National Assessment of Career and Technical Education: Final Report to Congress* (Washington, DC: US Department of Education, 2014).
2. For more detail and research on inequality and youth unemployment, see chapter 4.

Chapter 1

1. William C. Symonds, Robert B. Schwartz, and Ronald F. Ferguson, *Pathways to Prosperity: Meeting the Challenge of Preparing Young Americans for the 21st Century* (Cambridge, MA: Harvard Graduate School of Education, 2011).
2. National Commission on Excellence in Education, *A Nation at Risk* (Washington, DC: US Department of Education, 1983), 5.
3. Carnegie Forum on Education and the Economy, *A Nation Prepared: Teachers for the 21st Century* (Washington, DC: The Forum, 1986); National Governors' Association, *Time for Results: The Governors' 1991 Report on Education* (Washington, DC: NGA, 1986).
4. William T. Grant Foundation Commission on Work, Family, and Citizenship, *The Forgotten Half: Non-College Youth in America* (Washington, DC: William T. Grant Foundation, 1988).
5. Karen Levesque and Lisa Hudson, *Public High School Graduates Who Participated in Vocational/Technical Education: 1982–1998* (Washington, DC: US Department of Education, 2003).
6. "Table 9. Number of Persons Age 18 and Over, by Highest Level of Educational Attainment, Sex, Race/Ethnicity, and Age: 2011," National Center for Education Statistics, https://nces.ed.gov/programs/digest/d11/tables/dt11_009.asp.
7. Anthony S. Carnevale, Nicole Smith, and Jeff Strohl, *Recovery: Job Growth and Education Requirements Through 2020* (Washington, DC: Georgetown University Center on Education and the Workforce, 2013).
8. Ibid.
9. Jennifer Burrowes et al., *Bridge the Gap: Rebuilding America's Middle Skills* (Boston: Harvard Business School, 2014), http://www.hbs.edu/competitiveness/Documents/bridge-the-gap.pdf.
10. Organisation for Economic Co-operation and Development, *Learning for Jobs* (Paris: OECD Publishing, 2010); OECD, *Jobs for Youth* (Paris: OECD Publishing, 2009).

11. Jaison R. Abel, Richard Deitz, and Yaqin Su, "Are Recent College Graduates Finding Good Jobs?" *Current Issues in Economics and Finance*, 20, no. 1 (2014). More recent data suggests that with the recovery, the percentage of underemployed graduates has dropped to about 25 percent by age 29.

12. Carnevale, Smith, and Strohl, *Recovery*.

13. Anthony S. Carnevale, Stephen J. Rose, and Andrew R. Hanson, *Certificates: Gateway to Gainful Employment and College Degrees* (Washington, DC: Georgetown University Center on Education and the Workforce, 2012).

14. Grace Chen, "Community Colleges vs. State Schools: Which One Results in Higher Salaries?" *Community College Review*, January 6, 2017, https://www.communitycollegereview.com/blog/community-colleges-vs-state-schools-which-one-results-in-higher-salaries.

15. Mark Schneider, "The Value of Sub-Baccalaureate Credentials," *Issues in Science and Technology* 31 (2015), http://issues.org/31-4/the-value-of-sub-baccalaureate-credentials/.

16. Jaison R. Abel and Richard Deitz, "Do the Benefits of College Still Outweigh the Costs," *Current Issues in Economics and Finance*, 20, no. 3 (2014), https://www.newyorkfed.org/research/current_issues/ci20-3.html.

17. The last six paragraphs of this chapter draw substantially on the following article: Robert Schwartz, "The Career Pathways Movement: A Promising Strategy for Increasing Opportunity and Mobility," *Journal of Social Issues* 72, no. 4 (2016): 740–59.

Chapter 2

1. This section is adapted from Robert Schwartz, "The Pursuit of Pathways," *American Educator* 38, no. 3 (2014): 24–29.

2. "Table H124, Percentage of Public High School Graduates Who Earned at Least 2.0 Credits or at Least 3.0 Credits in the Occupational Area, 2009," National Center for Education Statistics, https://nces.ed.gov/surveys/ctes/tables/h124.asp.

3. Michael Webb, with Carol Gerwin, *Early College Expansion: Propelling Students to Postsecondary Success, at a School Near You* (Boston: Jobs for the Future, 2014); Andrea Berger et al., *Early College, Continued Success, Early College High School Initiative Impact Study* (Washington, DC: American Institutes for Research, 2014).

4. The Linked Learning approach and certification encompasses NAF academies, California career academies, and other models. For more information, see www.linkedlearning.org.

5. Barry Schwartz, "More Isn't Always Better," *Harvard Business Review*, June 2006, https://hbr.org/2006/06/more-isnt-always-better.

6. See Barry Schwartz's TED talk on "The Paradox of Choice": https://www.ted.com/talks/barry_schwartz_on_the_paradox_of_choice.

7. Thomas Bailey, Shanna Smith Jaggars, and Davis Jenkins, *What We Know About Guided Pathways* (New York: Community College Research Center, Teachers College, Columbia University).

8. "AACC Pathways: The Pathways Project," American Association of Community Colleges, http://www.aacc.nche.edu/Resources/aaccprograms/pathways/Pages/default.aspx.

Chapter 3

1. Race to the Top is the federal program launched with ARRA (American Recovery and Reinvestment Act) funds to stimulate the economy.
2. This paragraph draws on the Tennessee New Skills for Youth Needs Assessment document prepared by JFF for the state.
3. "General Information," Cookeville High School, http://www.cookevillecavaliers.com/information/index.shtml.
4. For more information about Cookeville High School pathways, see http://www.accteam.org/cookeville-high-school-cte.html.
5. For more information, see https://www.tn.gov/thec/topic/sails.
6. Ashley A. Smith, "Evidence of Remediation Success," *Inside Higher Ed*, April 5, 2016, https://www.insidehighered.com/news/2016/04/05/tennessee-sees-significant-improvements-after-first-semester-statewide-co-requisite.
7. "CTE State–Model Programs of Study," Delaware Department of Education, http://www.doe.k12.de.us/Page/2016.
8. See more on the Delaware Tech career pathway and work-based learning experience in chapter 5. "Delaware Tech Programs of Study," Delaware Technical Community College, https://www.dtcc.edu/academics/programs-study.
9. "CTE State–Model Programs of Study," Delaware Department of Education.
10. For more information, see https://www.pltw.org.
11. See the Innovation Generation website as well as all the resources available to high school students and especially to those whose schools are part of Innovation Generation: http://innovationgenerationohio.com/. See also: "College Credit . . . While Still in High School," Columbus State Community College, http://www.cscc.edu/community.
12. See more about Youth CareerConnect and other federal policy streams in chapter 7.
13. For more information, see http://www.wonderfuleducation.org.
14. For more information, see http://www.wonderfulcollegeprepacademy.org and http://www.wonderful.com/social-responsibility/education.
15. Rhonda Barton, *What School and District Leaders Can Do to Prepare Rural Students for a Brighter Future* (Portland, OR: Education Northwest, 2015).

Chapter 4

1. Sections of this chapter are drawn from Nancy Hoffman, *Let's Get Real: Deeper Learning and the Power of the Workplace* (Boston: Jobs for the Future, 2015).
2. Andrew Sum et al., *The Plummeting Labor Market Fortunes of Teens and Young Adults* (Washington, DC: Metropolitan Policy Program at Brookings Institution, 2014).

3. Mellissa S. Gordon and Ming Cui, "Positive Parenting During Adolescence and Career Success in Young Adulthood," *Tijdschrift: Journal of Child and Family Studies* 24, no. 3 (2015): 762–71.

4. Sum, *Plummeting Labor Market Fortunes.*

5. Ibid.

6. Ibid.

7. Commonwealth of Massachusetts, Executive Office of Labor and Workforce Development, "Massachusetts Adds 13,000 Jobs in January," March 9, 2017, http://lmi2.detma.org/lmi/news_release_state.asp.

8. Nicoya Borella, Chris Jurek, and Lindie Martin, *The Young Adult Labor Force in Massachusetts* (Hadley, MA: UMass Donahue Institute, Economic & Public Policy Research, 2016).

9. Anthony P. Carnevale, Andrew R. Hanson, and Artem Gulish, *Failure to Launch: Structural Shift and the New Lost Generation* (Washington, DC: Center on Education and the Workforce, 2013).

10. Ibid.

11. Hoffman's own post–high school summer job in a hundred-woman typing pool in the un-air-conditioned Newark, New Jersey, courthouse gave her great impetus to study hard in college and find a career as something other than a typist. See the description of the ethnographies of work course in chapter 5.

12. Mark Whitehouse, "How Trump Has Changed the Financial Outlook for 2017," *Bloomberg View*, December 19, 2016, https://www.bloomberg.com/view/articles/2016-12-19/how-trump-has-changed-the-financial-outlook-for-2017.

13. Raj Chetty et al., *The Fading American Dream: Trends in Absolute Income Mobility since 1940*, NBER Working Paper 22910 (Cambridge, MA: National Bureau of Economic Research, 2016).

14. Jason DeParle, "Harder for Americans to Rise from the Lower Rungs," *New York Times*, January 4, 2012, http://www.nytimes.com/2012/01/05/us/harder-for-americans-to-rise-from-lower-rungs.html.

15. For a review of these studies, see Julian B. Isaacs, "International Comparisons of Economic Mobility," in *Getting Ahead or Losing Ground: Economic Mobility in America*, ed. Ron Haskins, Julia B. Isaacs, and Isabel V. Sawhill, (Washington, DC: Brookings Institution, 2008).

16. Sum, *Plummeting Labor Market Fortunes.*

17. Robert Halpern, "Supporting Vocationally Oriented Learning in the High School Years: Rationale, Tasks, Challenges," *New Directions for Youth Development* 134 (2012): 85–106.

18. Ibid., 89.

19. Ibid., 91.

20. Paul Smith, "The Means to Grow Up: Reinventing Apprenticeship as a Developmental Support in Adolescence," *International Journal of Lifelong Education* 28, no. 6 (2009).

21. Allan Collins, Ann Holum, and John Seely Brown, "Cognitive Apprenticeship: Making Thinking Visible," *American Educator* (1991), 96–97.

22. See the OECD Glossary of Statistical Terms.

23. Ibid.

24. Tim Bartik and Brad Hershbein, "College Grads Earn Less If They Grew Up Poor," W. E. Upjohn Institute, http://www.upjohn.org/sites/default/files/pdf/hershbein-bartik-degrees-of-poverty.pdf; Robert D. Putnam, *Our Kids: The American Dream in Crisis* (New York: Simon and Shuster, 2015); Robert D. Putnam, *Bowling Alone: The Collapse and Revival of American Community* (New York: Simon and Shuster, 2000).

25. Adam Gamoran, "The Future of Educational Inequality: What Went Wrong and How Can We Fix It?" *Resources*, July 11, 2015, http://wtgrantfoundation.org/resource/the-future-of-educational-inequality-what-went-wrong-and-how-can-we-fix-it.

26. David J. Deming, *The Growing Importance of Social Skills in the Labor Market*, NBER Working Paper No. 21473 (Cambridge, MA: National Bureau of Economic Research, 2015).

27. Annette Lareau, *Unequal Childhoods: Class, Race, and Family Life, 2nd ed.* (Oakland: University of California Press, 2011).

28. Ibid., 3.

29. Ibid.

30. This summary is drawn from Nancy Hoffman, "Guttman Community College Puts 'Work' at the Center of Learning: An Approach to Student Economic Mobility," *Change: The Magazine of Higher Learning* 48, no. 4 (2016): 14–23.

31. Bartik and Hershbein, "College Grads."

32. Ann Coles, *The Role of Mentoring in College Access and Success* (Washington, DC: Institute for Higher Education Policy, 2014).

33. Borella, Jurek, and Martin, *Young Adult Labor Force*, 1.

Chapter 5

1. "Work-Based Learning Continuum," College & Career Academy Support Network, University of California, Berkeley, http://casn.berkeley.edu/resource_files/work_based_learning_continuum.pdf.

2. See more on NAF and Linked Learning in chapter 2. See more on P-TECH in chapter 6.

3. This summary is based on Tobie Baker-Wright, "Career Pathways: Preparing Youth for STEM Futures," STEM Ready America, http://stemreadyamerica.org/article-career-pathways.

4. This summary is drawn from Nancy Hoffman, "Guttman Community College Puts 'Work' at the Center of Learning: An Approach to Student Economic Mobility," *Change: The Magazine of Higher Learning* 48, no. 4 (2016): 14–23.

5. One way that the original plan has been set awry by students is that a full 40 percent of students are choosing the "liberal arts" major rather than one of the four career-focused

guided pathways (urban studies, business administration, IT, and human services) that the college designed as the default choices.

6. John Bowe et al., eds., *Gig: Americans Talk About Their Jobs* (New York: Broadway Books, 2001).

7. Charlotte Cahill, *Making Work-Based Learning Work* (Boston: Jobs for the Future, 2016).

8. Maureen E. Kenny et al., "Preparation for Meaningful Work and Life: Urban High School Youth's Reflections on Work-Based Learning 1 Year Post-Graduation," *Frontiers in Psychology* (2016): 2.

9. National Association of Colleges and Employers, *Job Outlook 2015* (Bethlehem, PA: National Association of Colleges and Employers).

10. For a rundown on perceived and real barriers, see Charlotte Cahill and Sheila Jackson, *Not as Hard as You Think: Engaging High School Students in Work-Based Learning* (Boston: Jobs for the Future, 2015).

11. Anne Stanton, private communication, January 11, 2017.

12. These numbers are not consistent across cities; Chicago, New York, and Los Angeles are fourteen- to twenty-four-year-olds; Boston's figure is high school students alone.

13. Kenny et al., "Preparation for Meaningful Work and Life."

14. This section draws on interviews Nancy Hoffman conducted with students and teachers in Delaware's first cohort of manufacturing students. The content appeared in a JFF blog; see Nancy Hoffman, "High School Is Where Manufacturing Careers Start in Delaware," *Voices for Opportunity JFF Blog*, November 15, 2016, http://www.jff.org/blog/2016/11/14/high-school-where-manufacturing-careers-start-delaware.

15. See more on the Wonderful Company in chapters 3 and 6.

16. Thad Nodine, *Job Shadowing in Agriculture* (Oakland, CA: Jobs for the Future, 2016).

17. Thad Nodine, *Skills Mapping in the Central Valley* (Oakland, CA: Jobs for the Future, 2016).

Chapter 6

1. Learning for Jobs (OECD, Paris 2010) and an ongoing study of comparative VET systems conducted by the Center for International Education Benchmarking at the National Center on Education and the Economy (NCEE).

2. See Nancy Hoffman, *Schooling in the Workplace* (Cambridge, MA: Harvard Education Press, 2011).

3. Charlotte Cahill and Sheila Jackson, *Not as Hard as You Think: Engaging High School Students in Work-Based Learning* (Boston: Jobs for the Future, 2015).

4. Brandon Busteed, "America's 'No Confidence' Vote on College Grads' Work Readiness," Gallup Blog, April 24, 2015, http://www.gallup.com/opinion/gallup/182867/america-no-confidence-vote-college-grads-work-readiness.aspx.

5. However, the business community, especially the major national business organizations, has played a key role over the last twenty-five years in supporting education reform,

especially the movement to raise academic standards in our schools. A group of corporate CEOs led by Louis V. Gerstner of IBM came together with a bipartisan set of governors in 1996 to create Achieve, the organization that led the call for the creation of Common Core State Standards. In the late 1980s, another major business organization, the Committee for Economic Development, issued a series of reports calling for greater investments in education coupled with fundamental reforms. During the last decade, national organizations like Business Roundtable and the US Chamber of Commerce have also voiced opinions on education reform.

6. Craig Giggi et al., *The Skills Gap in U.S. Manufacturing 2015 and Beyond* (Washington, DC: Deloitte and the Manufacturing Institute, 2015).

7. For more on these two states, see their state spotlights in chapter 3 and the policy showcases in chapter 7.

8. For more information, see https://www.illinoisworknet.com/ilpathways/Pages/STEMLE.aspx.

9. For more information, see http://nationalnetwork.org.

10. Read more about Guttman in chapter 5.

11. Read more about Columbus State in chapter 3.

12. For more information, see http://bostonpic.org.

Chapter 7

1. This chapter is updated, adapted, and expanded from Charlotte Cahill, Nancy Hoffman, Amy Loyd, and Joel Vargas, *State Policies for Sustaining and Scaling 9–14 Career Pathways: Toward a Policy Set for Pathways to Prosperity* (Boston: Jobs for the Future, 2014).

2. For the most up-to-date details of 2016 policy advancements supporting stronger career learning in K–12 in all states, see Association for Career and Technical Education and Advance CTE, *State Policies Impacting CTE: 2016 Year in Review* (Silver Spring, MD: Advance CTE, 2016).

3. Adapted from New Skills for Youth application. The text of the executive order can be found at http://news.delaware.gov/2016/08/11/governor-markell-announces-initiative-to-expand-pathways-to-prosperity-program.

4. At this writing, Massachusetts is developing a policy and funding stream for career-focused early colleges. Some states have provided waivers or special legislation targeted at early college models. For example, New York State amended its Aid to Localities Budget Bill in 2014 to allow higher education partners participating in an early college high school or P-TECH program to set a reduced rate of tuition and/or fees, or to waive tuition and/or fees entirely. The expectation is that most participating community colleges will waive tuition.

5. The National Association of State Directors of Career Technical Education Consortium, *The State of Career Technical Education an Analysis of State CTE Standards* (Silver Spring, MD: NASDCTE, 2013).

6. Tennessee has done impressive work to eliminate programs, modernize remaining ones, and make comprehensive information widely available. "Career Clusters," Tennessee Department of Education, http://www.tennessee.gov/education/topic/career-clusters.

7. CCP replaces Ohio's Post-Secondary Enrollment Options program and all alternative dual enrollment programs previously governed by Ohio Revised Code Chapter 3365. Governor Kasich signed H.B. 487 into law on June 16, 2014. The CCP program is operational as of the 2015–16 school year.

8. "All Things Jump Start," Department of Education: Louisiana Believes, https://www.louisianabelieves.com/courses/all-things-jump-start.

9. "Jump Start Internship Guidelines," Department of Education: Louisiana Believes, http://www.louisianabelieves.com/docs/default-source/jumpstart/jump-start-internship-guidelines.pdf?sfvrsn=2.

10. Rennie Center for Education Research & Policy, *Student Learning Plans: Supporting Every Student's Transition to College and Career* (Cambridge, MA: Rennie Center for Education Research & Policy, 2011); see https://careertech.org/tennessee; Caralee J. Adams, "Career Mapping Eyed to Prepare Students for College," *Education Week*, March 23, 2012, http://www.edweek.org/ew/articles/2012/03/23/26career.h31.html.

11. Most state counseling mandates are funded through local tax levy funds. Thirteen states and Puerto Rico provide state funding to support mandated counseling services. For more information, see http://www.counseling.org/docs/licensure/schoolcounselingregs2011.pdf?sfvrsn=2.

12. Carol Miller Lieber, *Personal Opportunity Plans* (Quincy, MA: Nellie Mae Education Foundation, 2014).

13. As of 2011, twenty-nine states, the District of Columbia, Puerto Rico, and the Virgin Islands mandate the provision of school counseling services in public elementary and/or secondary schools; twenty-four of these mandate school counseling at all levels.

14. "ICAP: Individual Career and Academic Plans," Boulder Valley School District, http://bvsd.org/icap/Pages/default.aspx.

15. "Academic & Career Planning (ACP)," Wisconsin Department of Public Instruction, http://acp.dpi.wi.gov.

16. See, for example, Robert Halpern, *Youth, Education, and the Role of Society: Rethinking Learning in the High School Years* (Cambridge, MA: Harvard Education Press, 2013).

17. For more information on these issues, see Charlotte Cahill and Sheila Jackson, *Not as Hard as You Think: Engaging High School Students in Work-Based Learning* (Boston: Jobs for the Future, 2015).

18. "Wage and Hour Division," US Department of Labor, https://www.dol.gov/whd/regs/compliance/whdfs71.htm.

19. The good news, however, is that interest in apprenticeship is growing. While still seen largely as a pathway to employment for adults in the traditional trades, a small and growing movement is taking place both to modernize apprenticeship offerings to include health

and IT, for example, and to open more apprenticeship opportunities to youth. One attraction of apprenticeships is that they can be targeted to encourage students to enter high-demand fields where employers are eager for trainees. See "Has the First Job Disappeared? Connecting Young Workers to Employers and Career-Building Work Experiences," Aspen Institute, https://www.aspeninstitute.org/events/first-job-disappeared-connecting-young-workers-employers-career-building-work-experiences; Brian Sodoma, "My First Job: How Part-Time Work Pays Off for Teens—And Employers," *Forbes BrandVoice*, September 12, 2016, http://www.forbes.com/sites/gapincthiswayahead/2016/09/12/my-first-job-how-part-time-work-pays-off-for-teens-and-employers/#6031373d21e8.

20. "Innovation Grant," Delaware Department of Education, http://www.doe.k12.de.us/Page/431.

Chapter 8

1. CCSSO, *Opportunities and Options: Making Career Preparation Work for Students* (Washington, DC: CCSSO, 2014).

2. The Bridgespan Group, *The Strong Field Framework* (San Francisco: James Irvine Foundation, 2009).

3. Advance CTE, *Putting Learner Success First: A Shared Vision for the Future of CTE* (Silver Spring, MD: Advance CTE, 2016).

4. This section is adapted from Robert Schwartz, "The Career Pathways Movement: A Promising Strategy for Increasing Opportunity and Mobility," *Journal of Social Issues* 72, no. 4 (2016).

5. See, for example, Anthony S. Bryk and Uri Treisman, "Make Math a Gateway, Not a Gatekeeper," *Chronicle of Higher Education*, April 18, 2010, http://www.chronicle.com/article/Make-Math-a-Gateway-Not-a/65056.

6. Accenture, Burning Glass, and Harvard Business School, *Bridge the Gap: Rebuilding America's Middle Skills* (Boston: Harvard Business School, 2014).

7. For more information, see www.careerwisecolorado.org/.

8. Nancy Hoffman and Robert Schwartz, *Gold Standard: The Swiss Vocational Education and Training System* (Washington, DC: National Center on Education and the Economy, 2015).

ACKNOWLEDGMENTS

Although this book has only two authors, it depends on and reflects the work of our extraordinary colleagues on the Pathways to Prosperity Network team at Jobs for the Future (JFF) and in the field. We are especially grateful to Amy Loyd, JFF Associate Vice President, and Charlotte Cahill, Associate Director, for their substantive contributions to the work and for their helpful review of two key chapters. Others on the team whose work we have drawn upon are Marty Alvarado, Adelina Garcia, Kyle Hartung, Sheila Jackson, Daniel Trujillo, Joel Vargas, and Tobie Baker-Wright. We have also benefited enormously from the support of past and current leaders at Jobs for the Future, especially former CEO Marlene Seltzer and current CEO Maria Flynn. We have also been fortunate to be able to draw on the excellent editing skills and good humor of two members of JFF's Communications team, Sophie Besl and Carol Gerwin, without whose expertise and commitment there would be less clarity and more long sentences.

The Pathways Network came into being in response to the 2011 Pathways to Prosperity report issued by the Harvard Graduate School of Education. Bob Schwartz would like to thank his two report coauthors, Professor Ronald Ferguson of the Harvard Kennedy School, and William Symonds, now at Arizona State University. He would also like to acknowledge the very strong support for the Pathways project provided by former Dean Kathleen McCartney and current Dean Jim Ryan.

We also owe a debt of gratitude to two other organizations that afforded us the opportunity to study high performing vocational systems in Europe and Asia. In 2010 we spent three months at the Organization for Economic Cooperation and Development (OECD) as part of the study team responsible for Learning for Jobs, a sixteen-country review of the ways in which participating countries support the preparation of young people for work and careers. We would especially like to thank Senior Analyst and Project Leader Simon Field for including us on the study team. In 2014, we were invited by the National Center on Education and the Economy (NCEE) to take part in an international benchmarking study of vocational education and training, and in particular to produce a report on the Swiss system. We would like to thank NCEE President Marc Tucker and Vice President Betsy Brown Ruzzi for their support of the Swiss study and for their leadership of the larger benchmarking project. We would also like to acknowledge the friendship and invaluable contributions of Dr. Ursula Renold, former director of the federal office that oversees the Swiss vocational education and training system and current Director of Education System Research at the KOF Swiss Economic Institute at ETH Zurich. She organized our several Swiss visits, served as our tour guide to the system, and introduced us to Swiss thinking about how young people best grow up and find careers.

While the Pathways Network has been mostly self-funded since its inception in 2012, the Noyce Foundation was an early and sustained supporter, providing key grants at each stage of the Network's development. We would especially like to thank Noyce Board Chair Ann Bowers for her belief in the importance of this work and her continuing encouragement. More recently the Pathways Network has benefited from a generous grant made through Harvard by the James and Judith K. Dimon Foundation. We are grateful to the Dimons and to the Foundation's Executive Director, Abby Jo Sigal, who has become a colleague in the work as well as a funder.

Finally, this book would not have happened were it not for the encouragement of Doug Clayton, Publisher and Director of the Harvard Education Press (HEP). We have both enjoyed a long working relationship with HEP, Nancy as an author or editor of five previous HEP books, Bob as a contributor to seven edited volumes and as chair of the HEP Advisory Board for several years. Doug has been a wonderfully supportive partner in bringing this book to market, and for that we are deeply grateful. Finally, we celebrated our forty-sixth marriage anniversary while writing this book and want to acknowledge one another's good humor throughout the process.

ABOUT THE AUTHORS

Nancy Hoffman is a senior advisor at Jobs for the Future (JFF), a national nonprofit in Boston focused on improving educational and workforce outcomes for low-income young people and adults. Hoffman came to JFF in 2001 to lead the national Early College High School Initiative, which is funded by the Bill & Melinda Gates Foundation. Hoffman is the cofounder of the Pathways to Prosperity State Network with Bob Schwartz. Hoffman has held teaching and administrative posts at Brown, Temple, Harvard, the Fund for the Improvement of Postsecondary Education (FIPSE), the Massachusetts Institute of Technology, and elsewhere. She has served as a consultant for the education policy unit of the Organisation for Economic Cooperation and Development (OECD). Her 2011 book Schooling in the Workplace: How Six of the World's Best Vocational Education Systems Prepare Young People for Jobs and Life (Harvard Education Press) introduced a US audience to the range of VET systems abroad. Hoffman and Schwartz are the authors of Gold Standard: The Swiss Vocational Education and Training System, published by the National Center on Education and the Economy in 2015.

Hoffman holds a BA and PhD in comparative literature from the University of California, Berkeley. Other books include Spenser's Pastorals: The Shepheardes Calendar and Colin Clout (1977); Women's True Profession: Voices from the History of Teaching (2003); and several coedited volumes, including Double the Numbers: Increasing Postsecondary Credentials for Underrepresented Youth (2004), Minding the Gap: Why Integrating High School with College Makes Sense and How to Do It (2007), and Anytime, Anywhere: Student-Centered Learning for Schools and Teachers (2016), all published by the Harvard Education Press. Hoffman serves on the Massachusetts Board of Higher Education as well as on the board of North Bennet Street School, which offers intensive, hands-on training in traditional trades and fine craftsmanship. She coteaches a course at the Harvard Graduate School of Education on new pathways to college and career.

Robert B. Schwartz joined the faculty of the Harvard Graduate School of Education (HGSE) in 1996, where he has served, successively, as Lecturer, Professor of Practice, Academic Dean, Francis Keppel Professor in Educational Policy and Administration, and Senior Research Fellow. Prior to joining the HGSE faculty, Schwartz served in a variety of roles in education: high school teacher and principal, education advisor to the mayor of Boston and the governor of Massachusetts, assistant director of the National Institute of Education, executive director of the Boston Compact; and education program director at the Pew Charitable Trusts. From 1997 to 2002, Schwartz served as founding president of Achieve, Inc., a nonprofit organization created by governors and corporate leaders to help improve performance in US schools.

Since 2010, Schwartz has participated in two OECD studies, Learning for Jobs and Strong Performers and Successful Reformers, and contributed chapters to four prior Harvard Education Press volumes: Teaching Talent (2010), Surpassing Shanghai (2011), The Futures of School Reform (2012), and Improving the Odds for America's Children (2014). In 2011, he coauthored an influential report calling for more attention to career and technical education, Pathways to Prosperity: Meeting the Challenge of Preparing Young Americans for the 21st Century. In 2012, he cofounded, with Nancy Hoffman, a national network of states and regions that was formed to act upon the analysis and recommendations outlined in the Pathways report, now called the Pathways to Prosperity Network.

INDEX